Contents

Chapter 10

How to Market and Promote your E-Commerce Store

Steps to take to Market and Promote your E-Commerce Website

Register your Business

Build SEO friendly E-commerce Site to gain Online presence

The impact of Social Media Sites on Promotion of Online Stores

Marketing your E-commerce Site by paid Advertisements

How to Advertise your E-Commerce Site with Google (Google Ads)

How to Advertise your E-commerce site on Facebook

Promoting your E-commerce Site from known to unknown people

Advertising on bigger E-commerce Websites

Getting People review your Products

Advertising your Store through Radio and Television Channels

Chapter 1

Introduction to E-commerce Website

It is important to find out the possibility in building e-commerce website that you can use for your 24 hours in a day business. It is a standard functional website that people from your locality or outside your country can buy products from. When they place order, you and your team supply the products they need to them.

People spend money online. People in the United States spent $602 billion online in 2019. And that was before the Coronavirus changed everyone's shopping habits. In the first month after the pandemic started, e-commerce sales grew by 49%. Any business owner that stays offline is missing out on their piece of those profits.

E-Commerce websites have made many entrepreneurs from different parts of the world rich. Business owners who were struggling in their businesses before have found their feet because they are making good amount of money by selling through their websites. People are really making it big by displaying and selling through their self-hosted websites.

Do you have idea of how much entrepreneurs make from E-commerce businesses which they execute through their websites? Do you know how much they make from such websites every year? In 2019, ecommerce was responsible for around $3.5 trillion in sales and is expected to hit $4.9 trillion by 2021. In the US alone, ecommerce represents over 10% of retail sales and that number is expected to grow by nearly 15% each year. From that analysis, e-commerce is taking over the world. As a result of this, you need to learn how to build such kind of website. It can yield you money from business owners who do not have the time to build such kind of website.

In this book, I will guide you with updated information on how to build this kind of website to make sales on the internet. You do not need to kill yourself over some codes to get this job done. I will be teaching you using WordPress and WooCommerce collaboration approach. So, just follow my guide in a step by step way and you will surely get it right at the end of the teaching. I am your teacher on this topic, so, please listen and apply my guide.

What is an E-Commerce Website?

E-Commerce, also known as e-Business, or electronic business, is simply the sale and purchase of services and goods over an electronic medium, like the Internet. It also involves electronically transferring data and funds between two or more parties. Simply put, it is online shopping as we commonly know it. Ecommerce can also be defined as the process of purchasing of available goods and services over the internet using secure connections and electronic payment services.

E-Commerce started way back in the 1960s when organizations began to use Electronic Data Interchange (EDI) to transfer documents of their business back and forth. The 1990s saw the emergence of online shopping businesses, which is quite a phenomenon today. The first-ever online purchase was a Sting CD, sold by US retailer, NetMarket on 11 August 1994. "In 2020, eCommerce sales are expected to account for 15.5 percent of retail sales worldwide."- Oberlo.in

An e-commerce website is that website that allows the sell and purchase of services and goods over an electronic medium, like the Internet. E-Commerce websites are online portals that facilitate online transactions of goods and services through means of the transfer of information and funds over the Internet. In the early days, e-commerce was done partially through emails and phone calls. Now, with a single website, anything and everything that a transaction needs, can be executed online.

Top e-commerce websites known globally include amazon.com, walmart.com, ebay.com, alibaba.com, taobao.com and etsy.com. These are the giants among other e-commerce websites known globally. There are some that operate locally in their individual countries. Amazon is the king of all e-commerce websites. The company has large arms and heart. As a result of this, the company is making money and making people rich. There are thousands if not millions of people that depend on Amazon and they work from home to that e-commerce website and earn their living through the website as well.

History of E-commerce and E-commerce Website

One of the most popular activities on the web is shopping. E-commerce became functional in the year 1991 when internet was approved for commercial use. Since that year, thousands of entrepreneurs embraced that and have been making sales through their websites. In the other words, e-commerce websites came into existence in the year 1991.

At first, the term ecommerce meant the process of execution of commercial transactions electronically with the help of the leading technologies such as Electronic Data Interchange (EDI) and Electronic Funds Transfer (EFT) which gave an opportunity for users to exchange business information and do electronic transactions. The ability to use these technologies appeared in the late 1970s and allowed business companies and organizations to send commercial documentation electronically.

Although there have been sales through the internet, there was a huge change and outbreak in higher sales in the year 2000. This made many businesses in United States of America to start building ecommerce sites to make sales in higher volume.

In that same year 2000, the dot-com collapsed. This was a big slap on the faces of many business companies. Many felt bitter as such affected their businesses and hence closed their ecommerce websites.

Irrespective of the collapse of the dot-com websites in 2000, many brick and mortar businesses still stood firm. They rebuilt their websites and still run their online stores. The "brick and mortar" retailers recognized the advantages of electronic commerce and began to add such capabilities to their websites (e.g., after the online grocery store Webvan came to ruin, two supermarket chains, Albertsons and Safeway, began to use e-commerce to enable their customers to buy groceries online). By the end of 2001, the largest form of ecommerce, Business-to-Business (B2B) model, had around $700 billion in transactions.

We cannot finish discussion on the history of e-commerce websites without mentioning the early beginners Amazon.com and eBay.com. These are big ecommerce websites who are really making our world great today. These two companies located in United States have been a source of livelihood to many people inside and outside United States of America. The companies have intelligent managers. Amazon started with selling of books but today is selling a lot and products and services that cut across many departments. Amazon.com stands out among all ecommerce websites.

Types of E-commerce Websites

E-commerce websites are of different types. The types of ecommerce websites are as follow:

- Business-to-Business
- Business-to-Consumer
- Consumer-to-Consumer
- Consumer-to-Business

Business-to-Business (B2B): Electronic transactions of goods and services between companies. Example: A business sells SAS (Statistical Analysis System) products to other businesses. It can be a business transaction between Amazon and eBay as an example.

Business-to-Consumer (B2C): This is online transactions of goods and services between companies and consumers. Example is when you buy a book from Amazon. If you bought this my book from amazon.com that means your carried-out business-to-consumer transaction with the company.

Consumer-to-Consumer (C2C): Electronic transactions of goods and services between consumers, mostly through a third party. Example: You sell your old smartphone on eBay or Olx to another consumer. ebay.com is among this type of ecommerce website. People sell their used book through eBay.

Consumer-to-Business (C2B): Electronic transactions of goods and services where individuals offer products or services to companies. Example: A Social media influencer offers exposure to their online audience in exchange for a fee. Some growing businesses that sell online, pay social media celebrities for their ecommerce websites to be showcased on the pages of the celebrities.

Note: A large ecommerce website can run up to two type of transaction explained here or more.

Why you need to learn E-commerce Website Building Skill

There are reasons you need to learn how to build e-commerce websites. The reasons are as follow:

- It can fetch you money as a website builder. When you acquire the skill on how to build e-commerce websites, people can hire you to build for them. There are many business owners today who need the services of ecommerce website builders. When you build for such people, you earn money.

- It gives you the sense of belonging in the world of technological development which we find ourselves today. Unlike people who do not possess any tech skills, sometimes they feel that they are left behind in our world of today. When you learn how to build ecommerce website, it gives you sense of belonging. Even when people discuss something on tech skill, you can contribute as a person who possess skill in that area.

- It puts you ahead of many people. There may be an interview held by a company and you happen to be among the job seekers. When you mention that you can build an ecommerce website in the ear of the interviewer, it can be an added advantage to you. That can make you get that job. You never can tell if they have needed someone that will help them build one until you appear.

- Learning a skill on how to build an e-commerce website can save you money. If you decide to have your own website tomorrow, instead of paying someone else to build a website for you, you can do that on your own. When you build it, you build it to your taste and not giving the job to someone who may be in a haste to build it and thereby not giving you the best. You need to learn the simple way to get the job done which after you can do it on your own and save yourself the money you may give to someone else. Just pay attention to my teaching in this book and you will get it done the right way.

Chapter 2

Choosing a Domain Name and Hosting

This is the real thing. It is where the journey of creating website starts from. If you have no domain name, there is no way you will own a website. The first thing you must do in creating an e-commerce website for yourself or someone else is to choose a domain name.

A domain name is that name which you want your website to answer. A domain name is your website name. A domain name is the address where internet users can access your website.

The first thing is to pick a domain name and another thing is to check whether the domain name is available for your proposed e-commerce website to answer. Yes, that is it. If the domain name has been taken by someone else, you cannot answer that domain name. Example, for the website www.amazon.com, the domain name is "amazon". What that implies is that there cannot be two "amazon" on the web. That unique name has been given to the company by domain name registrars.

Fig 2: Picture showing amazon as a domain name

What you should know in Choosing Domain name

There are things you need to know before you choose a domain name. These are as follow:

- A domain name is combination of letters that forms a unit. What I mean is that the letters that form the domain name cannot be separated from each other. For example, you can have a domain name as "donsmart" but cannot have a domain name as "don smart". That space is not allowed.

- A domain name once chosen and registered cannot be changed. Before you register a domain name, you should know that it cannot be changed until it expires. Otherwise, you register another domain name for yourself, and that will be double expenses.

- Make your domain name short and easy to capture. It is better you make your domain name short and something that will be easy for buyers from your e-commerce website to remember. If you want to make it long, just do it in a way that people can remember it. It is better to have a website URL as "www.smartlearn.com" than having "www.uzfsyulearn.com".

Can you see the difference in the two? The domain name "smartlearn" can easily be remembered by buyers than "uzfsyulearn". Buyers will find it difficult to pronounce that second domain name. This will make them not to visit the site if they want to visit it again later. Because they could not pronounce the name, they could not visit the site as they forgot the domain name.

Domain Name Registration

You must first register your domain name through any website hosting company. It is this hosting company that will make sure that your website is always online. In the other words, they will make sure that your files are stored in their server. Any time people visit your website, these files appear as products and posts in their eyes.

There are several website hosting companies you can host your website with. When you visit their websites, you first check with their tool on the website to know if the website name you want to take is available. If it is, you can proceed with the registration.

At the end, you pay the company and then they register your domain for you. The website hosting company on their own then take the money for domain name registration, for giving you domain name, and for keeping your files and web active on the internet.

Some hosting companies allow people to pay for at least one-year hosting of their websites. But in the recent time we have seen some changes in the duration of hosting. There are some registrars of websites that can allow you to pay for 1 to 3 months period. An example of such domain name registrar (also the same with website hosting company) is Inter Server with website URL as www.interserver.net.

Fig 2.1: Inter Server homepage

If you are a beginner, you can start with this website hosting company. Inter Server is cool and fine for people who do not know much about web building. With this company, you can just subscribe for 3 months to experiment on what you have learned and what you are going to learn. After that you can decide whether to extend it and continue making use of the site.

There are many website hosting companies today. In United States alone, there is over 900 website hosting companies in the country. It is your choice to make on the one you want to use to host your website. The prices paid varies as well. It is like you deciding on the price to sell an item to people and another seller deciding on the price to sell that same product in his own shop.

Some website hosting companies are as follow:

- GoDaddy
- Google Cloud Platform
- Amazon Web Services (AWS)
- BlueHost
- Squarespace
- Namecheap
- HostGator
- Automattic
- Wix Hosting
- Liquid Web
- DreamHost
- Weebly
- Digital Ocean
- InMotion Hosting
- Rackspace
- Peedam Hosting
- Linode
- Leaseweb
- Media Temple
- EGI Hosting

- Cogeco Peer

- Network Solutions

- SiteGround

-HostMonster

-Psychz Networks

- iPage

-A2 Hosting

- SoftLayer

- Smart Web

- Hostway

- Inter Server

So out of the above listed website hosting companies, you are to make your choice on the one to use. They are all confirmed domain name registrars. In the next heading, I will be taking you on the practical approach on how to register a domain name through any of the hosting companies.

Practical: Step-by-Step Guide in Registering your Domain Name

Step 1

Visit the website of any of the above listed website hosting companies. If you do not know the direct link or the URL of the hosting company, you can search for the name through Google. The website of BlueHost is https://www.bluehost.com, that of GoDaddy is https://uk.godaddy.com, and that of Inter Server is https://www.interserver.net.

Step 2

Check for the domain name availability. You are to search through the homepage of the hosting company you visit to know if that name you want to give your website is available. There is usually a search box provided for you to do so on the website.

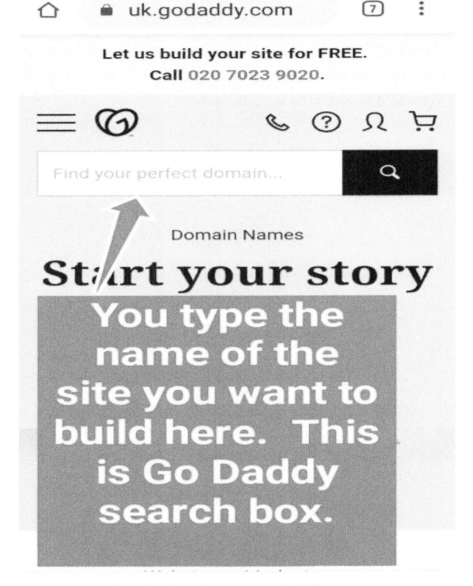

Fig 2. 1: Searching for domain name availability

If you search and the name has been taken, you have to try another name. You keep trying until you get the one that is free. But sometimes, if a domain name has been taken, the person that took it can still resell it to you if he or she has not built complete website on it. But he or she will do that at higher price if you really need it. Example is the experience I hard when I wanted to register techkindle before I finally chose teachkindle.

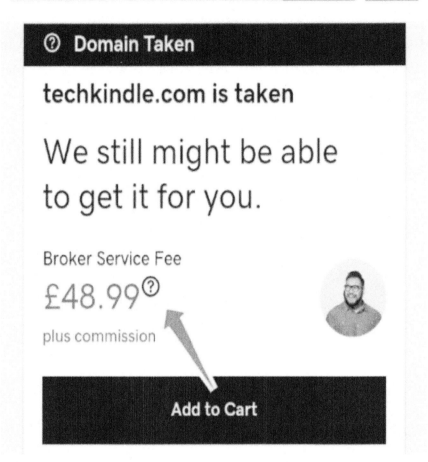

Fig 2. 2: When someone has taken your domain name choice but wants you to pay higher to get it.

Step 3: Building with the Available Domain Name

Because the name I wanted to use for my website was not available and I didn't want to pay that amount of money to get it from the person that first registered it, I then try another name.

At this stage I chose to try another domain name called "teachkindle". If I tried and the name was free, I went on with it. But if it was not available, I would keep on trying. Once the domain was available, I saw a message like "CONGRATULATIONS YOUR DOMAIN IS AVAILABLE".

Step 4: Sign Up with the Hosting Company

Since the name you want your website to bear is available, you then signup with the website hosting company you want to use. In the signup, you fill in the major information required from you. If you already had account with the website hosting company, you can sign in using your email address you have with them and your password.

I will show you sample. When I hosted recently, I used Inter Server hosting company. I didn't not use GoDaddy again though I searched for domain name using their platform. You can still do the same using Inter Server website hosting company. I signed up with them before I could continue to make payment for my domain name "teachkindle".

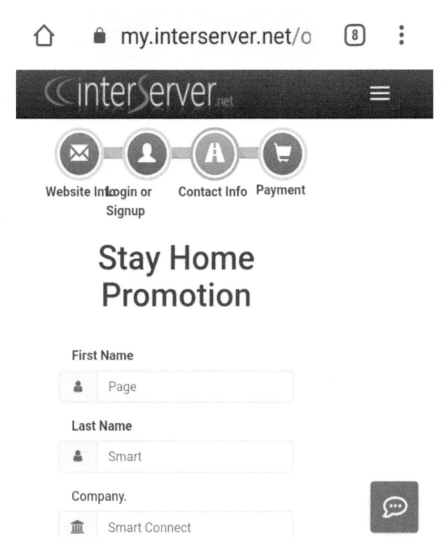

Fig 2.3: The sign up in progress

Once you sign up for an account with the company successfully, they will send you email within a short time on how to continue with your purchase of the domain name. You can get an email in this format:

"Hello!

Your InterServer account has been created.

Login Name Smart*********014@gmail.com

This sign up came from IP address **7.21*.84.**7

You can login to your account by visiting https://my.interserver.net

You can reset your password visiting https://my.interserver.net/password.php

--

Thank You,

Team Interserver"

Step 5: Login and Choose a Package

So, since you know that a particular domain you finally decided your website will answer is free, you are to login to the website of the same web hosting company. You will see "web hosting" on top or by the side of the website. Click on that and then search for the domain name again in the search box for verification purpose. The congratulations message showing you that the name is free will come up again.

You will be shown some packages. The packages vary by price. The reason is because each package has some features that make them higher than the other. In Inter Server for instance the packages the hosting company has are STANDARD WEB HOSTING, RS ONE, RS TWO, RS THREE, RS FOUR, RS FIVE, ASP.NET WEB HOSTING, WORDPRESS MANAGED HOSTING, and STAY HOME PROMOTION. As a beginner, I advise you go for Standard web hosting. Other website hosting companies have terms they use to categorize their packages also.

As you select any package, you will be shown how much you are to pay for a package per duration you want to own the domain. You can decide to own the domain for 3 months or a year.

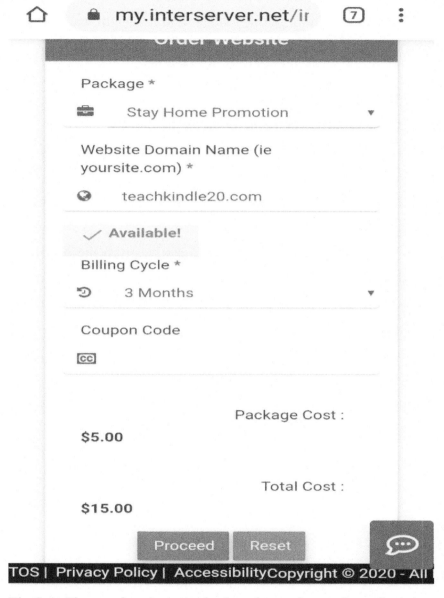

Order Website

Package *

Stay Home Promotion

Website Domain Name (ie yoursite.com) *

teachkindle20.com

✓ **Available!**

Billing Cycle *

3 Months

Coupon Code

Package Cost :

$5.00

Total Cost :

$15.00

Proceed   Reset

Fig 2.4: Picture showing standard package chosen for a domain and the amount to pay

Note: The domain name teachkindle20.com was chosen for this particular demonstration. In other stages and this entire teaching, we will be using **teachkindle.com** for most of our illustrations.

Step 6: Billing and Payment

This is the next step. Then when you proceed to the next step after choosing your plan, you will be shown an invoice of how much you will pay.

You will be given some options on the method you want to use to make the payment. Some hosting companies has up to 3 payment options while others do have less. You can be given the options to pay with card, direct deposit to the bank, or pay with PayPal. But some domain name registers have the option of pay with card and Payment with PayPal account.

In pay with card option, you input your debit or credit card number and the CVV number at the back of the card. CVV mean Card Verification Value. It is usually a 3-digit number at the back of credit or debit card.

Fig 2.5: Image showing the CVV of a Master Card

After you enter the information for your account to be debited, you will get a security code sent to you by your bank through your phone number asking for your approval for your account to be debited. A box will be provided for you by the hosting company to enter the code. Once you enter the code correctly in the box, your account will be debited.

You will get a confirmation email in your inbox confirming your payment. The hosting company will also send you details on how to login to your control panel and install any program/application to start building your own website. The details to be sent to you for you to be able to log in to your email is your username or email and password. You are to keep them safe.

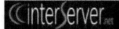

Payment Approved

Dear Page Smart,

Your payment of $6.99 was approved and successfully applied to your balance for your Domains.

Invoice ID	4493201
Invoice Description	(Repeat Invoice: 18744140) Whois Privacy for Domains 425304
Invoice Date	2020-05-19 13:53:26
Invoice Amount	5.00
Domains ID	425304
Domain Hostname	teachkindle.com
Domains Type	10039

Invoice ID	4493200
Invoice Description	(Repeat Invoice: 18744139) .com Domain Name Registration
Invoice Date	2020-05-19 13:53:26
Invoice Amount	1.99
Domains ID	425304
Domain Hostname	teachkindle.com
Domains Type	10039

Please let us know if you have any comments or suggestions on how to improve our service by emailing support@interserver.net.

Thank You,
InterServer Team.

Fig 2.5: Confirmation email received after paying for hosting a domain

The caption is a confirmation message I received from a website hosting company after paying for my package using credit card.

Note: Your payment may not go through after you put in the card details required from you to make payment for your domain name and hosting. You can get an error message. The error message can be because your card has not been verified. The message can be in this format:

Error! CC Disabled! Payment type credit card is currently unavailable. Remove the credit card(s) you have on file and add them again. If you continue having issues please contact us.

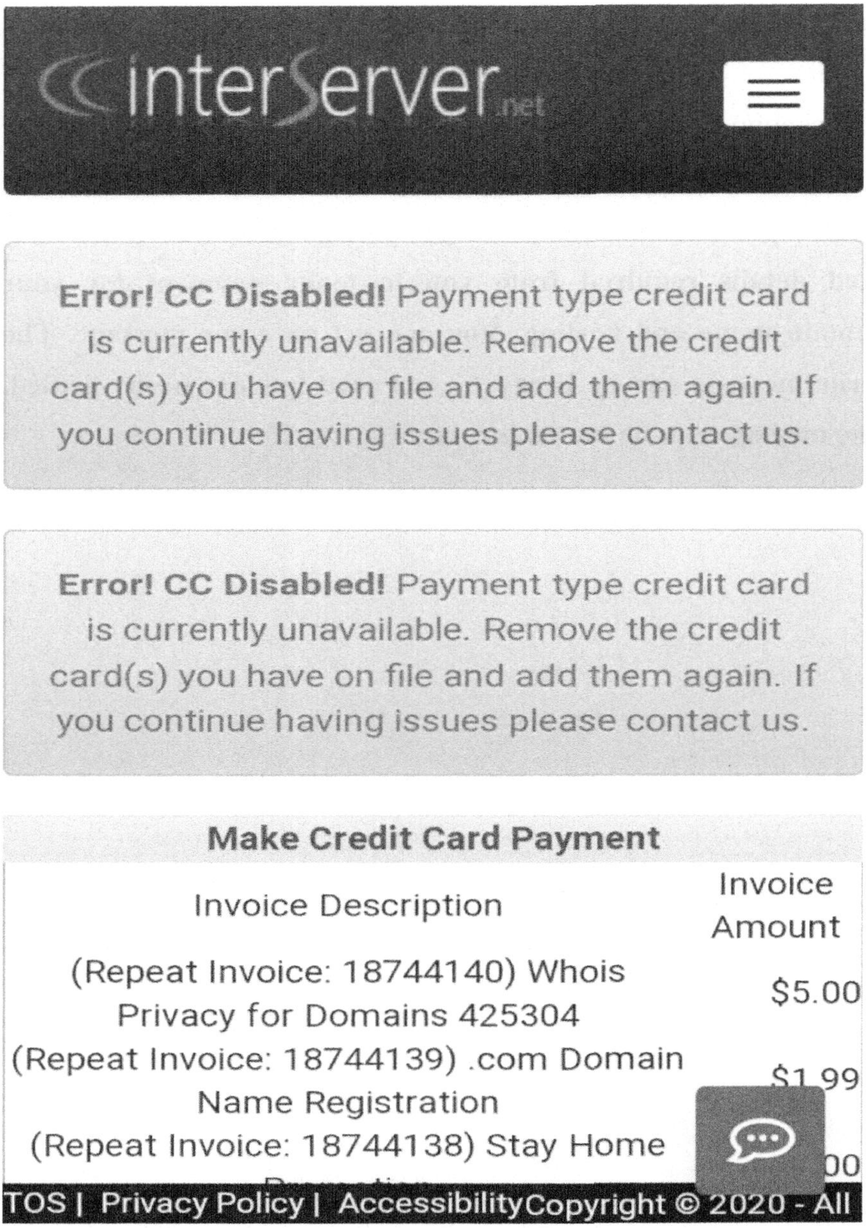

Error! CC Disabled! Payment type credit card is currently unavailable. Remove the credit card(s) you have on file and add them again. If you continue having issues please contact us.

Make Credit Card Payment

Invoice Description	Invoice Amount
(Repeat Invoice: 18744140) Whois Privacy for Domains 425304	$5.00
(Repeat Invoice: 18744139) .com Domain Name Registration	$1.99
(Repeat Invoice: 18744138) Stay Home	00

TOS | Privacy Policy | AccessibilityCopyright © 2020 - All

Fig 2.6: Error message after trying to pay for my domain hosting using card

To resolve the issue, the best thing is to write to their customer care. You will be responded to within 24 hours, but it depends on the hosting company. The customer care representative will guide you on what to do to resolve this. After this and you make another attempt to make your payment, it will go through without stress. If any error massage appears again, still write to them.

Conclusion

In this chapter, I was able to guide you through on step-by-step approach on how to host your website or domain. By host, I mean how to pay for a name you want your website to answer. Also, I taught you about some website hosting companies that can help you with the hosting. So, you are to choose from the many listed. Building a website is a simple thing. If you have any question or clarification you want from me, do not hesitate to write to me. My email address is at the last page or one of the last pages of this book.

Chapter 3

Installing WordPress and Account Setup through Control Panel

Let me throw a little light on what WordPress is before going deep on how to install it. It will help you understand better what the content management system is. It will also give you knowledge on the similarity it has with other software you might have used in your computer or mobile phones before now.

WordPress (WordPress.org) is a free and open-source content management system (CMS) written in PHP and paired with a MySQL or MariaDB database. Features include a plugin architecture and a template system, referred to within WordPress as Themes.

Historically, the CMS was originally created as a blog-publishing system but has evolved to support other types of web content including more traditional mailing lists and forums, media galleries, membership sites, learning management systems (LMS) and online stores. In terms of online stores, WordPress fits in properly in this so far you use the right theme. Using WordPress to create online store which is also called E-commerce website is what this book is about.

Fig 3: WordPress.org logo

In terms of number, WordPress is used by more than 60 million websites, including 33.6% of the top 10 million websites as of April 2019. It is one of the most popular content management systems used by website builders all over the world.

WordPress is easy to use, and it has good flexibility. Not only that, WordPress has many responsive themes in their system. You have thousands to choose from. It is your choice to select any from the many themes and start building your site from there.

A Step-by-step Guide on how to Install WordPress and Continue with Building of your Website

Step 1: Login to your Control Panel

After you have finished with your payment to the domain hosting company and your payment confirmed and approved, you will be sent a mail to the email address you filled with the domain hosting company. The email will contain the details you need to login to the control panel of your domain. Example of the mail can be seen below:

"ACCOUNT INFORMATION:

========================

Plan: Stay Home Promotion

Domain: teachkindle.com

IP Address: ***.72.**5.67

CPANEL LOGIN INFORMATION:

====================

https://webhosting34004.is.cc:9883

Username: teacgain

Password: ****b80*

FTP INFORMATION:

=================

FTP (SSL/TLS available):

***.72.**5.67

Username: teachkin

Password: ***L*7**"

You must first click on the link in that detail. Using the sample, I gave, you are to click on the link https://webhosting34004.is.cc:9883. The link will take you to a page requesting you enter the username given to you and the password also. Once you do that, you will be logged in to the control panel.

Do not worry too much about what control panel is. A control panel is the administration portion of your webhosting account. It is an interface that you access to administer all the aspects of your account. Control panel of a web is like that control panel in your laptop. It is the place where things can be changed and structured.

Don't be disturbed even if you do not understand the short description properly. What should be more important to you should be how to build a working e-commerce website at the end of this teaching.

With the given information, you can them login to your control panel.

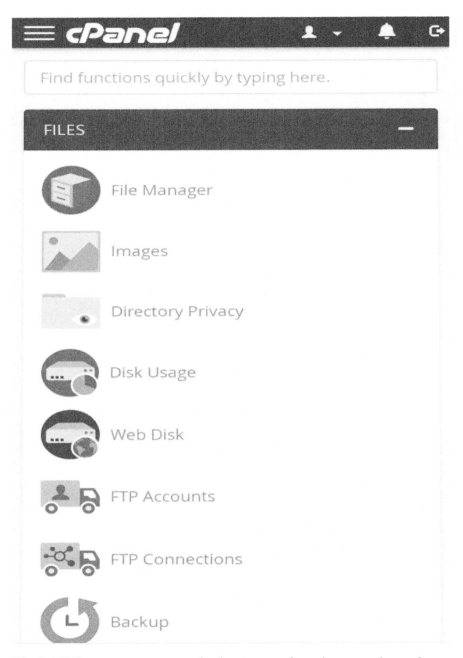

Fig 3.1 What appears as you login to your domain control panel.

Step 2: Install WordPress

After you have login to the Control panel using the details given to you by the website hosting company, scroll down to the section named "SOFTACULOUS APPS INSTALLER". In that section, click on the WordPress symbol.

Fig 3.2: WordPress Application in control panel

When you click on "WordPress" and the application opens, scroll down and click on "Install now". And once you do this a new page opens which requires you to fill some information.

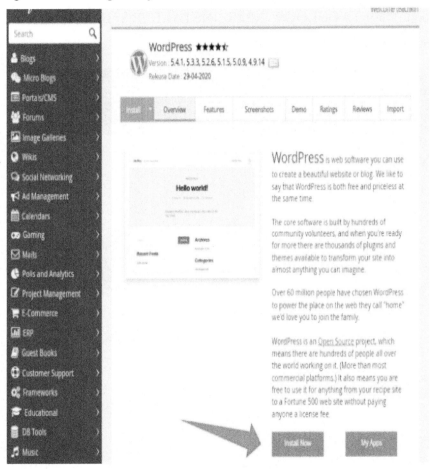

Fig 3.3: Click on the Install Now

Then fill the necessary details required from you. You must not fill in all the space, but the important boxes required of you to fill.

I want to make something clear to you, in the space of "In directory" do not fill anything there. You can still read the previous sentence again. Clear that space for everything to be empty (do not allow any letter to be there). The reason for doing this is so that you install the website in the root directory of WordPress.

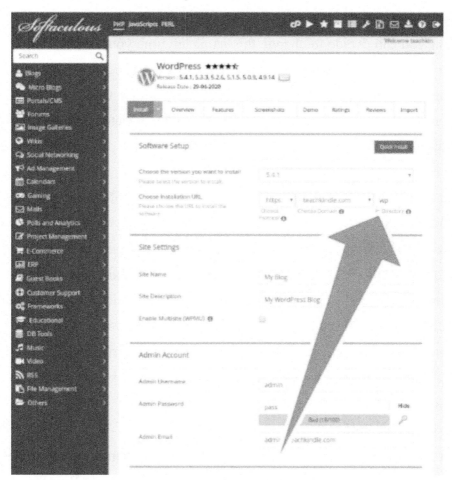

Fig: 3.4: Setting up WordPress (delete the "wp")

Using the image, you are to delete the "wp" and then leave the box empty.

Fill in the right information in the other boxes provided for you:

Site Settings Section

In the "Site Name" fill the name you want your website to answer. Using my own domain name which we have been using in this teaching, I can decide to fill my own "Site Name" as "Tech Kindle" or "Teach Kindle". The name to give the website is my choice.

But you can decide to change this name anytime you feel like doing so. That is the flexibility in building website. The only thing you cannot change is that website link (URL) which website hosting company gave you at hosting. For example, I cannot change my website (domain name) link www.teachkindle.com. It is permanent. It has been registered on the web worldwide.

In the "Site Description" you are required to describe your website shortly. So, delete that "My WordPress Blog" already put in the space by default and put few words that will tell people what your website is all about. Using my own website "teachkindle.com" I can input "TK Store". This is because I am going to build the site as an online store. When I have this in my description, it will send signal to visitors on what my website is all about whenever they visit.

For " Enable Multisite (WPMU)" do not tick the box. You are to leave it as it is.

Admin Account

In this section, you are required to fill in the name you will be known with on the website or as you login to your WordPress account after the final setup, password to be used to login to your WordPress, and email address to be used to receive email news and notifications from them (WordPress).

In the "Admin Username" you can type in your real name. You can also type in any name you like to answer.

I believe you have visited any website whereby you were shown the publisher's name on top of the page. The reason why that name shows as that is because that name was chosen as the admin name on a website run by a single person. In my own case, I can choose to put "William S. Page" as my "Admin Username".

In the " Admin Password " you are to fill in the password you will use to login into your site after setup. The password should be strong and should not be easily predicted by people. Please do not use your date of birth as your password. Also do not use your mobile phone number either.

Use a password that cannot be easily broken by hackers. You can write it down and put in a place you know people will not see it. Even if you forget your password tomorrow, you can reset it and a link to do that will be sent to your working email address.

For the "Admin Email" please do not use the email address already generated by WordPress system there. Do not make that mistake. In the image, you can see "admin@teachkindle.com" in that space filled in already. That was autogenerated. So, I will not use it. I didn't create any email like that.

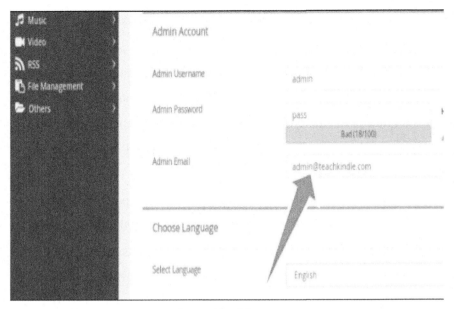

Fig 3.5: The autogenerated email address

Edit that email generated by the system and put your active email address. You can put your Gmail, Yahoomail, Hotmail, or any other email you make use of. It must not be a custom email. WordPress need that email to notify you of any changes or important news you need to know about their products. The admin section should not be played with as that can be used to help you recover your account if issues arise.

In the choose language section, just choose the language you want your website to be written in. There are many language options on WordPress. As of May 2020, there were 37 language options available in WordPress. Among these languages is English, Spanish, Chinese, German, Italian, Dutch, Greek, Hebrew, Arabic, Danish, Finnish, French, Croatian, Portuguese, Hungarian language and others.

Manage Plugin Sets

For this section, do not tamper with anything there. Just leave it as it is by default. When we are done with the installation of the WordPress, we can manage plugins from our dashboard. So, do not tick anything on "login Limit Attempts (Loginizer)", "Classic Editor" and "wpCentral - Manage Multiple WordPres".

Advanced Options

In the "Advanced Options" section, do not change anything there. Leave those options the way they are. With time when you master website building properly, you can make changes you want.

Stage 3: Theme Selection

There are many themes you can select in WordPress before you finally complete your installation. It is your choice to choose from the Plenty available themes. Themes give your website the beauty it is required to have.

In the "Select Theme" section, you are expected to make your selection. If the one you want to use does not appear first, click on the arrow pointing towards the right to see other themes. Keep on going until you see the theme you feel will fit the website you want to build. But if you do not see any which you have in mind, do not worry because you will be exposed to more themes in WordPress admin area after installation.

Fig 3.6: Arrow shows where to click when your choice of theme does not appear first

Also, if you already have the name of a WordPress theme you want to use, you can use the theme search box to search. Just put the name of the theme and hit search. The theme will pop up and you select it.

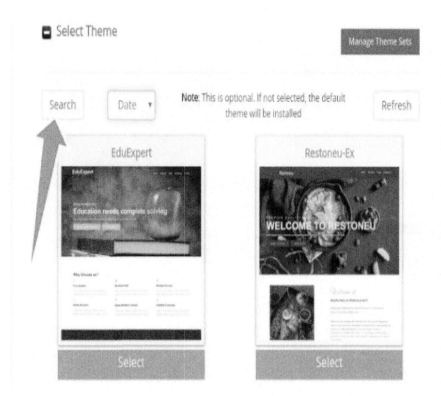

Fig 3.7: When you click on the search, a window will pop up and you type the name of the theme

Check through all the information you filled in the WordPress installation page. If you will forget your password or the email address you used in your WordPress, you can write them down or save them in any cloud application you make use of.

When you are sure that everything you filled is in order, there is something more you need to do before you hit install. At the bottom of the page, look very well and you will see "Email Installation Details to". In that box, fill in your email address you want WordPress to send your installation details to.

Fig 3.8: Type in your functioning email address there

When I built my first website, I forgot to fill that space. I waited for long expecting WordPress to send any installation details to my email address, but it didn't come. I later uninstalled the WordPress and reinstalled a new one filling everything correctly, that was when I got the details from them.

Installation details contains some information. The information is:

- Your website Path
- Your website URL
- Admin URL
- Admin Username
- Admin Password
- Admin Email
- MySQL Database
- MySQL DB User
- MySQL DB Host
- MySQL DB Password
- Update Notification: Enabled or Disabled
- Auto Upgrade: Enabled or Disabled
- Automated Backups: Enabled or Disabled
- Time of Installation

When you have verified every information you have entered and then select Install, the page loads and the installation is completed. Below is the similar page you will see:

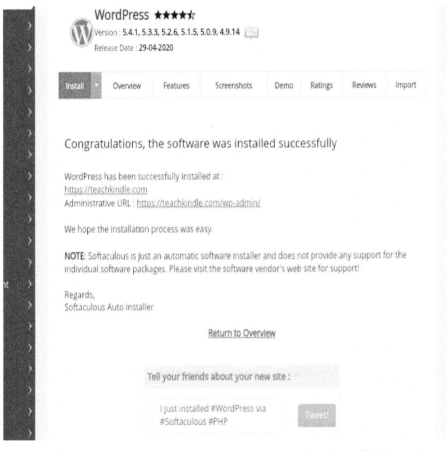

Fig 3.9: Picture shows next page that appears after installation

I used the word "similar" because my domain name is different from the one you will be using. As my own domain name is different and unique, that is why my administrative URL is unique.

You may ask what URL is? URL stands for Uniform Resource Locator. It is just a website link. In this sample, my administrative URL is https://teachkindle.com/wp-admin/. Once I type that in any browser, I can input my username and password, and login to my WordPress admin area.

So, for your own, once you installed WordPress after you have filled the necessary information required of you, your own admin URL will be https://your domain name/wp-admin/. Let us say your domain name is "uniquefood" your admin URL will be https://uniquefood.com/wp-admin/.

What will You do if after Installation your Website does not Load?

It is expected that once you put your email address where your installation details are to be sent and then hit "Install" and the installation is successful, your website suppose to start working immediately. If you visit "www.mywebsite.com" at that point, it supposes to load and open a new page.

If I visit my website www.teachkindle.com immediately after the installation is completed, it supposes to load just as I have in the picture:

Fig 3.1.1: Homepage of my newly created website

What to do when your Newly Created Website does not Load

If after the WordPress installation and your website does not load or you receive error message, there is something you can do. Without wasting much time, visit the website of the domain hosting company where you hosted your website.

Login in, and then write to them concerning the issue. They will respond to you within minutes on what caused the issue. At the end it will be resolved. Sometimes such issue occurs because the site has not been verified.

When I hosted my site teachkindle.com with Inter Server and installed WordPress for the site building, I got an error message when I visited that my website. I refreshed the page many times and the error message kept coming.

I then logged in to my account with Inter Server website and sent mail to them. They responded to me within few minutes explaining the cause of the error. I was instructed to verify my new domain that it is a rule from ICANN before my website would work. I did that and my website started loading fine.

Below is the message I got from my hosting company (Inter Server) on the issue:

"** Please note that failure to complete the process outlined below will lead to the suspension of your domain name. **

Dear Customer,

Please read this important e-mail carefully.

Recently you registered, transferred or modified the contact information for one or more of your domain name(s). ICANN requires all accredited registrars to verify your new contact information. You can read about ICANN's new policy at: http://www.icann.org/en/resources/registrars/raa/approved-with-specs-27jun13-en.htm#whois-accuracy.

teachkindle.com

In order to ensure your domain name remain active, you must now click the following link and follow the instructions provided:

http://approve.domainadmin.com/registrant/?verification_id=10892562&key=eUnUzdWKRy&rid=2833

Failure to follow the above link and complete this process will eventually lead to the suspension of your domain name(s).

If you have additional questions, please do not hesitate to get in touch.

Thank you for your attention,
InterServer Inc"

Chapter 4

New Theme Installation and Plugins

There are many themes in WordPress theme section. Irrespective of the number of themes available, some themes serve special needs. The theme you use for an ordinary blog site cannot serve the need of that needed to build an e-commerce website. As a result of this, you must install a new theme to be used for the building of your new e-commerce website.

The theme is something entirely different from the one we used when we were making WordPress installation from Control Panel. In the recent time, many developers have been working hard to create more themes so that the builders of e-commerce websites can choose from the many available themes. And as they do so, they make more money for creating such which add beauty to technology. It is all about business.

Before going further on this area of interest, it is important to let you know what a theme is. I know if you are a beginner you may be asking yourself question close to, what is a theme? So, without asking further I will tell you what a theme is in relation to website building.

A website theme is the overall look, feel and style of a website. This includes things like the color scheme, layout and style elements. Your website theme is a direct representation of your brand and has a direct impact on your users' experience.

A WordPress theme changes the design of your website, often including its layout. Changing your theme changes how your site looks on the front-end, i.e. what a visitor sees when they browse to your site on the web. Different themes suit different kinds of website. Out of thousands of themes in WordPress Theme Directory, you are to choose the one you believe suites the kind of website you want to build.

In building online stores or e-commerce websites which is where we are paying more interest on, there are themes that suit that kind of website. Example of the theme is Astra e-commerce theme. With this kind of theme, you can build beautiful e-commerce website.

A plugin is a piece of software containing a group of functions that can be added to a WordPress website. They can extend functionality or add new features to your WordPress websites. In building of an e-commerce website, we need some plugins including WooCommerce, payment gateway plugins (Example PayPal, Remita, WooCommerce Payment Gateway, and Instamojo), Elementor, Starter Templates, YITH WooCommerce Wishlist, and Customizer Search.

Installation of New E-Commerce Theme

After installation of WordPress through the control panel as discussed in the previous chapter, the next thing you are to do is to login to your WordPress dashboard. You remember that after the installation, you established WordPress account through the control panel.

You chose a username and password then. After that setup, you were given administrative URL to be used to access your WordPress dashboard. For example, mine is https://teachkindle.com/wp-admin. Your own will follow the format https://yourdomainname.com/wp-admin. You are to insert that link in your browser, then enter the username and password you chose to access your WordPress administrative area.

Step-by-step Guide in Installation of New E-Commerce Theme

The steps in carrying out this task is as follow:

- Login to your administrative dashboard using your username and password

With your username and password login to your admin area. First insert your administrative URL in a browser and then hit enter.

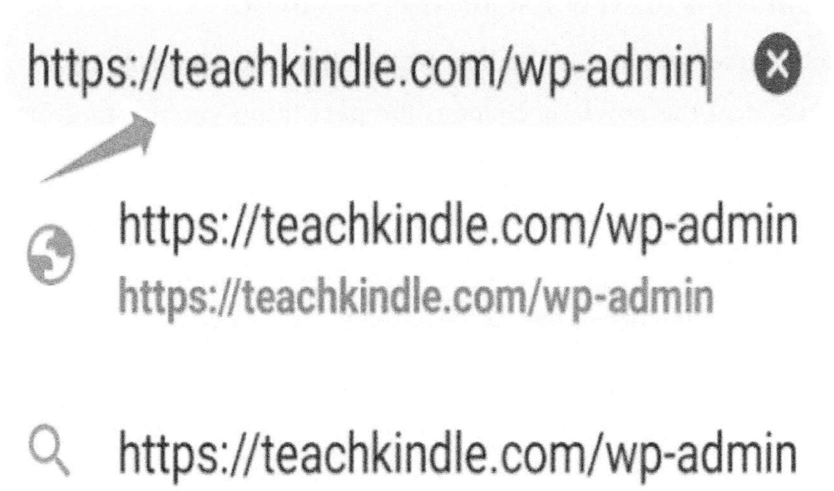

https://teachkindle.com/wp-admin

https://teachkindle.com/wp-admin
https://teachkindle.com/wp-admin

https://teachkindle.com/wp-admin

Fig 4: Inserted administrative URL in a browser

After you inserted the administrative URL and hit "enter" on your keyboard or "search" as the case may be, a login page opens. Insert your username or email, and your password to login to the dashboard of WordPress.

Fig 4.1: Logging in to WordPress admin dashboard

- Select Appearance

As you login to the dashboard, one of the screen options you will see is Appearance. You are to select it.

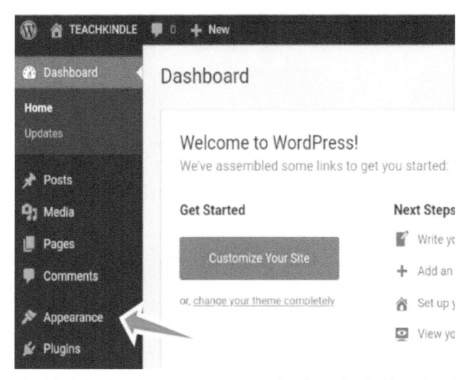

Fig 4.2: Selecting Appearance screen option from the dashboard
- Select Themes

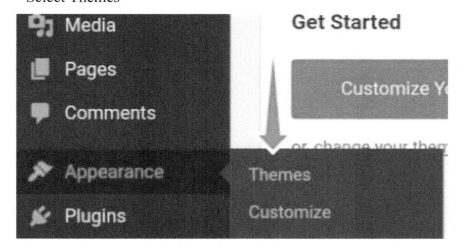

Fig 4.3: Selecting Theme option from the dashboard

The theme appears as one of the functions under Appearance.

- Select Add New

When you select Add New by the right, a new search box opens. This box allows you to search for any theme you want to use on your website.

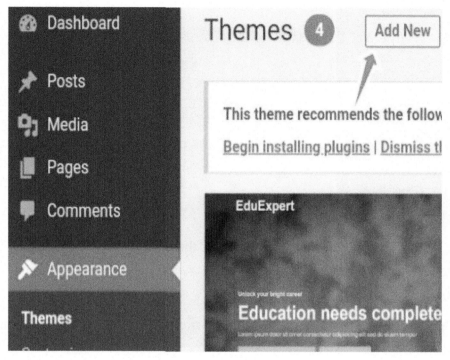

Fig 4.4: Arrow shows the location of Add New

- Type Astra in the space

When you type Astra in the search box in as much as the search option is to search with keyword, Astra theme will show up.

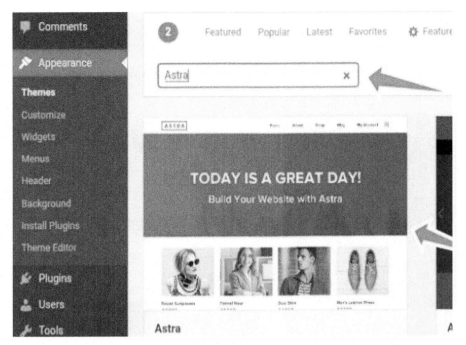

Fig 4.5: The picture shows the Astra theme shows up when Astra was typed in

- Select the Astra theme that shows up

As you click on the Astra theme, you are to see the clearer view of the theme.

- Install and activate the theme

When you select the theme, look on top of the next page that opens. You will see "Install" on top. Click on that and the theme gets installed on your website.

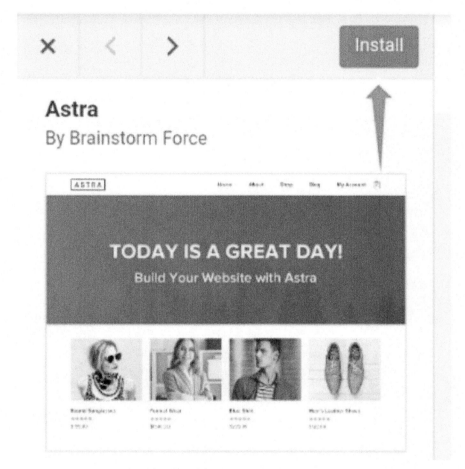

Fig 4.6: Arrow points at Install

Also, when you click on "Install" another word shows up on the same spot. The word is "Activate". Click on the Activate and the theme gets activated on your website. When you click on Activate and the activation is successful, you will see a congratulatory message. The message reads "Thank you for installing Astra"

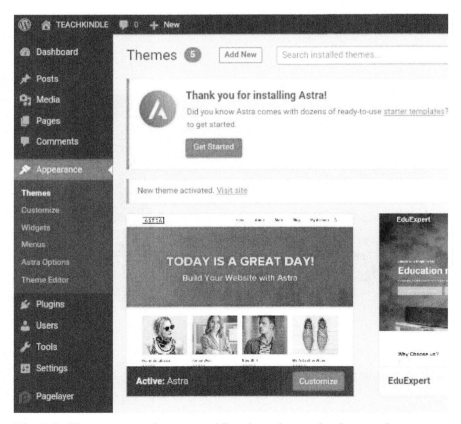

Fig 4.7: The congratulatory notification shown in the caption.

As you finish with the installation and activate of the theme, you will see a notification suggesting that you install plugins that will help the theme function well. If you look at the image of fig 4.7, on the screenshot is the message that reads "This theme recommends the following plugins: Contact Form 7 and One Click Demo Import. Begin installing plugins". If you click on the keyword "Begin installing plugin" which is hyperlinked, you will be taken to the plugins section to install those plugins. But do not worry much because we are starting the next subheading from here.

Step-by-Step Guide in Installing Plugins

You are to first install the plugins recommended by the Astra theme. This is the continuation from the previous subheading.

So, click on the keywords "Begin installing plugin" which is hyperlinked, and you will be taken to the plugins section to install those plugins. Note that this shows up after we installed and activate Astra theme. If that does not show up, you may see the notification telling you that Astra theme comes with starter templates, you can click on the button "Get Started" to install the plugin.

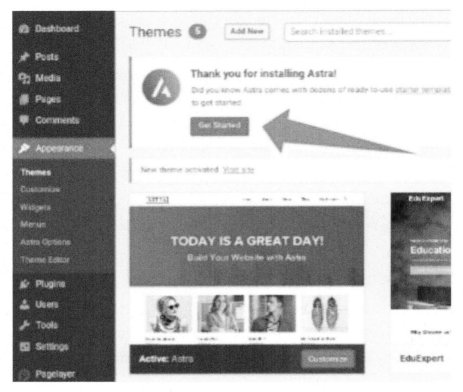

Fig 4.8: Arrow points at "Get Started"

You are to click on the "Get Started" to install Starter Template plugin

When the theme recommends that you should install more than one plugin once, I advise that you follow the instrument. Example is the one shown in my image below.

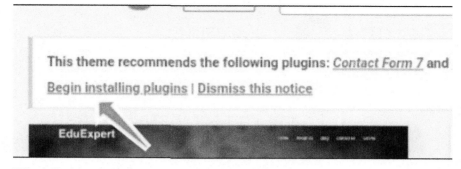

Fig 4.9: Arrow points at Begin installing plugins

You are to click on the "Begin installing plugins" to be taken to the right page.

Installing and Activating Starter Template

There are two ways we can use to install and activate starter template plugin in WordPress. We can decide to start from the notification we got after installing and activating Astra theme or We can start from Admin dashboard.

Installation and Activation of Starter Template Plugin from the Notification

From the notification we got after the installation of Astra theme, do the following:

- Click on "Get Started"

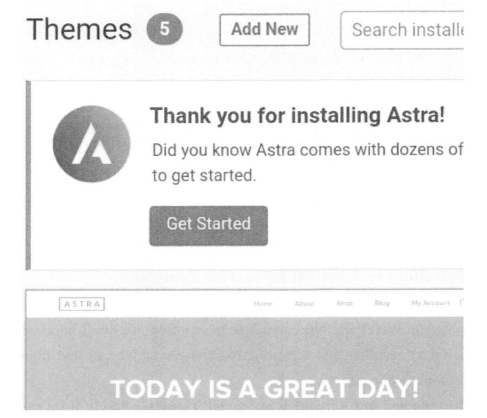

Fig 4.1.1: Click on the Get Started button

- Select Elementor

Among the page builders that shows up when you click on Get Started, just select Elementor. When you select Elementor, a new page opens showing you some temples.

Fig 4.1.2: Arrow points at Elementor

- In the top right-hand side click the drop-down button and select eCommerce.

This will show you some available eCommerce templates. Some are free to use while some are not. But we are going to do our building with one of the free ones.

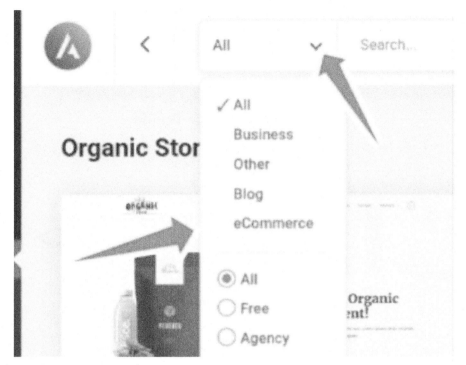

Fig 4.1.3: Picture shows the dropdown to select before choosing eCommerce option

- Select any of the free ecommerce templates

I will advice you choose the one called "Brandstore" for the purpose of this teaching. It has the logo designed with "DNK". But you are free to choose anyone you feel like using.

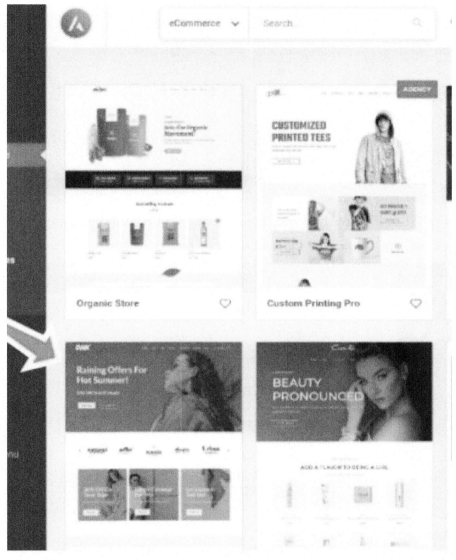

Fig 4.1.4: You are to click on that template to select it, and it is the template called Brandstore

- Click on " Important Complete Site"

This will make the template make a complete change to your entire website look.

Fig 4.1.5: Picture shows the position of "Import Complete Site"

- Click on "Import" in the new window that shows up.

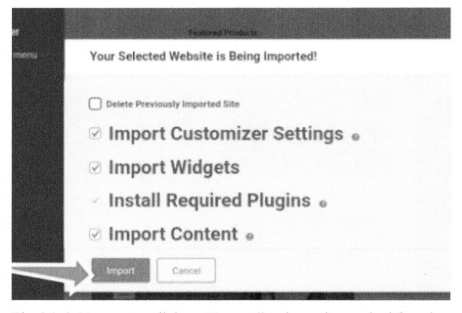

Fig 4.1.6: You are to click on "Import" to have the marked functions imported along

Once the importation is complete, you will see a congratulatory notification appear on your computer screen.

Example is the one that shows in on the caption below:

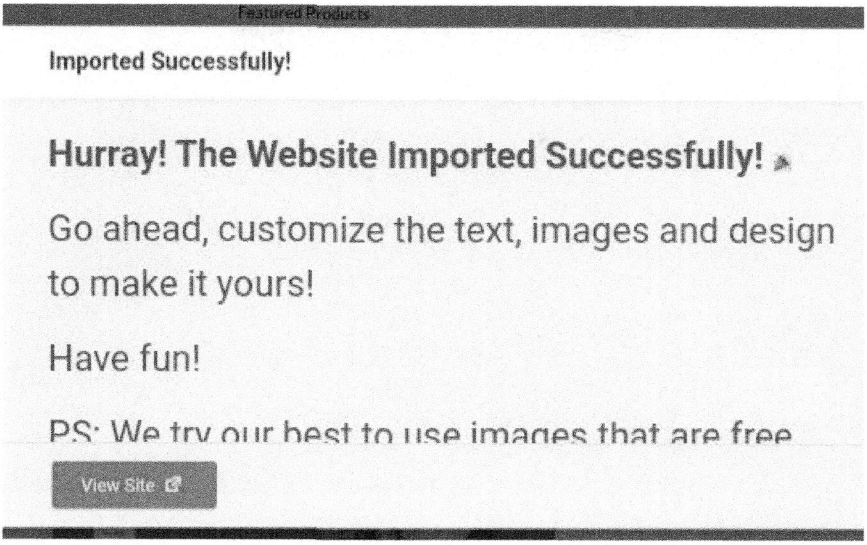

Featured Products

Imported Successfully!

Hurray! The Website Imported Successfully! ✈

Go ahead, customize the text, images and design to make it yours!

Have fun!

PS: We try our best to use images that are free

View Site ⧉

Fig 4.1.7: Congratulatory message after importation of a new template

When you click on "Visit Site" you will be taken to the homepage of your website where you will see the beautiful change the imported template has made which makes it appear like real ecommerce website.

Fig 4.1.8: The middle to top part of my website teachkindle.com after installing the e-commerce template

But it's a real ecommerce website, we just have to make few touches, and everything becomes completely set.

WooCommerce Plugin

WooCommerce a key plugin we need to build our online store. It is one of the most popular (if not the most popular plugin) used in building of ecommerce websites. It has great features that enables users to set up their electronic stores at ease. WooCommerce is fully customizable.

Fig 4.1.9: WooCommerce logo

WooCommerce is developer friendly, too. It is one of the fastest-growing e-commerce communities. The members of the online communities help one another sort issues out in times of difficulty.

The company has team of happiness engineers who work remotely from 58 countries providing customer support across multiple time zones. They also do great job to ensure that plugin work fine on WordPress sites. They test compatibility of their plugin with WordPress themes.

The payment section of WooCommerce is a simple one. The company accepts payment from Credit and Debit cards. Also, it allows you to set up account that allows buyers pay directly into your bank account. When the customers make payments, the company remits to your own bank account you fill with them. You can track your transactions from their dashboard.

WooCommerce Payments is currently available to U.S.-based merchants only. The company is actively planning future availability based on users' interest. The company is on the plan for gradual expansion.

Practical: Step-by-Step Guide in Installing and Activating WooCommerce Plugin

Most times when you install e-commerce theme through your WordPress admin area and the system recommends some plugins to install, WooCommerce plugin is usually installed with it. So if you see WooCommerce logo among the screen options on your admin dashboard, you do not need to install it again. But if it is not there, you must install it differently.

To install and activate WooCommerce plugin, follow the steps below:

- Login to the admin dashboard of your WordPress

If you are not logged in to the admin of section of your dashboard, please login. But if you have already logged in, visit the home of your dashboard.

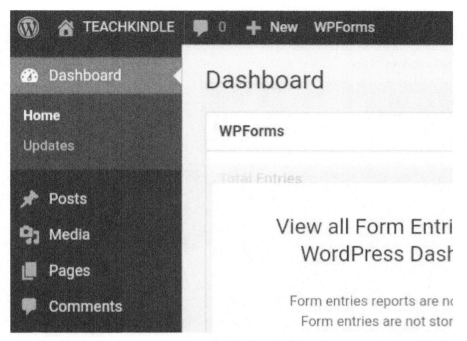

Fig 4.2.1: The homepage of my admin dashboard

- Click on Plugins

Plugins screen option is located after Appearance on the dashboard.
But some themes vary, just look for it and select it.

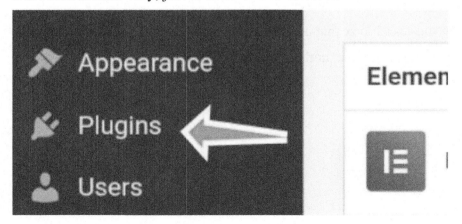

Fig 4.2.2: Arrow points at Plugins

- Select Add New

As you click on the plugins, there are other features that shows, just select Add New

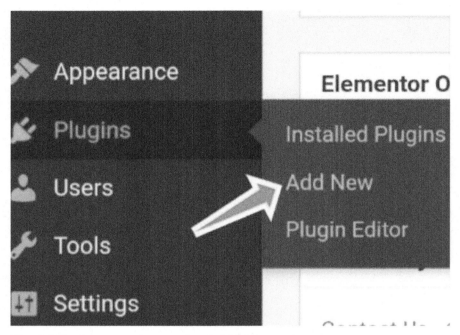

Fig 4.2.3: Arrow points at the Add New option

- Type in WooCommerce

In the search box that appears when you selected Add New, just type in WooCommerce, and the plugin will pop up.

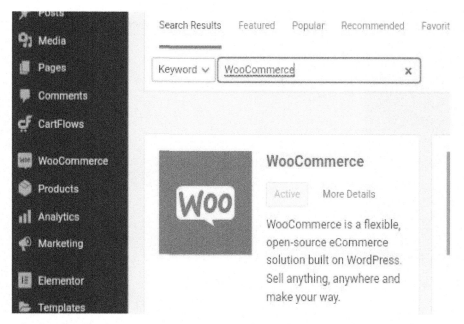

Fig 4.2.4: Typing in WooCommerce in the search box

From the picture above, the WooCommerce plugin is already installed on my WordPress, otherwise, the small button showing "Active" should have shown "Install". It should have been as below:

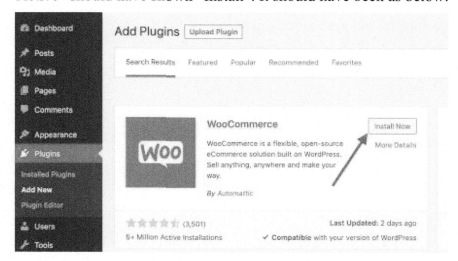

Fig 4.2.5: Fresh installation of WooCommerce plugin

- Click on Install Now on the plugin

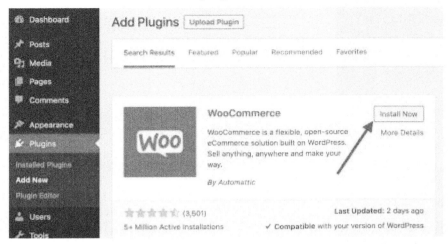

Fig 4.2.6: Arrow points at where to click

When you click on Install Now, you will be able to install the plugin. But if the WooCommerce plugin is already installed in your WordPress site as shown in Fig 4.2.4, you will not see this feature. So, no need going further. Just go to your admin dashboard and continue with some other building steps. Or wait until I start teaching on other areas for you to follow up.

- Click on Activate

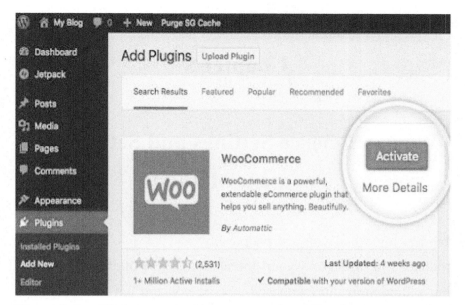

Fig 4.2.7: Click on Activate to make WooCommerce plugin functional

When you click on Activate and the activation is successful, you are good to go and can start setting up other areas. But, do not rush into it because I will guide you through on how to do it.

Note: We may be needing other plugins, but we will install them as we make our journey in this book. Enjoy the upcoming teachings!

Chapter 5

WooCommerce Settings and Setting Up Payment Methods

There is joy when you see people buy and be able to pay for the products you display on your online store. No matter how stunning your online store may appear to be, if you are not able to set up means through which customers can use to pay and you get credited in your bank account, it is rubbish. In fact, it is as bad as you have done nothing. We are to set up channels through which our customers can be able to make their payments.

This is where many beginners in online store building run into trouble. But never mind because I will detail everything completely for your adequate comprehension. You will learn how to carryout this task that give many online store dummies headache from beginning to the end. I am here for you so feel free to reach me through my email if you run into trouble as you get this job done. My email address is on one of the last pages of this book.

A good and sound online store can make up to a billion dollar for the owner of the online store. Amazon's online stores have made more than a billion dollar for Jeff Bezos, the owner of the stores.

But if the payment methods were not built well at the construction stages of these stores, there would have been no way payments would be made successfully. In fact, if you give this book another title "How to Build a Billion Dollar App", it is not bad because e-commerce sites which are web applications have made more than a billion dollars for many owners.

Setting up payment methods can be done using only the installed and activated WooCommerce plugin only. But depending on the kind of online store you want to build, there may be need for you to install another plugin for a company that receives online payment to collaborate with WooCommerce. We will get there later.

If for example you want to build an online local store in India that will only accept buyers from India alone, then there will be need for you to install and activate a plugin for a company's payment gateway in India. One that most Indians use is the one called Instamojo.

Instamojo is one of the top-rated payment gateway & e-commerce platform in India. It is trusted by 1200000+ Indian small businesses. It has really helped many online businesses in India.

If I am building an e-commerce website that will cover only a particular country in Africa as well, I have to search for a particular payment gateway that will help the owner get paid as well. There are many of such companies in different countries. So, no need for you to stress your brain much.

A good e-commerce website should have as many payment methods as possible. That will make buyers choose from the many available options. In this teaching, I will be making those options available. That will help us make more money from our online store.

Step-by-Step Guide in Setting up Payment Method using WooCommerce in United States

This method can be used in building online stores whose buyers are from United States. Because WooCommerce company has office in United States of America, it makes it much easier to process payments for business owners from the country.

To set up payment method with WooCommerce, take the following steps:

- Login to your WordPress admin Area or go to the dashboard

If you are already logged in to the WordPress, just go to the home of your Administrative dashboard.

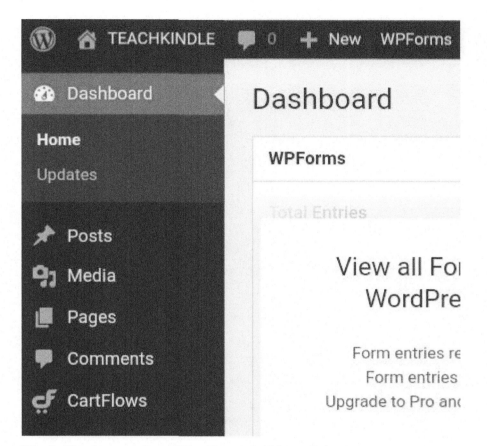

Fig 5: The home of my WordPress dashboard shown

- Click on WooCommerce screen option

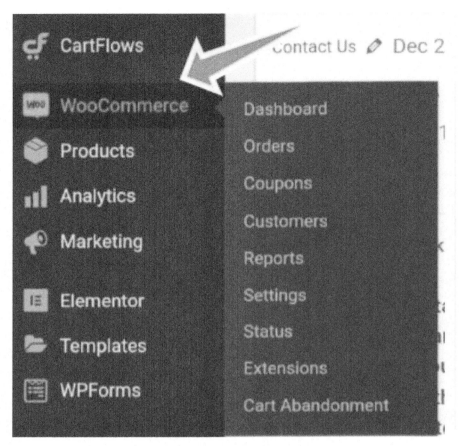

Fig 5.1: Arrow points at WooCommerce screen option

- Select Settings

When you select Settings, you are required to set up account with WooCommerce. In settings, you have some headings. These headings include General, Products, Shipping, Payments, Account and Privacy, Emails, Integration and Advanced. You are to click on each of the heading and make changes where necessary.

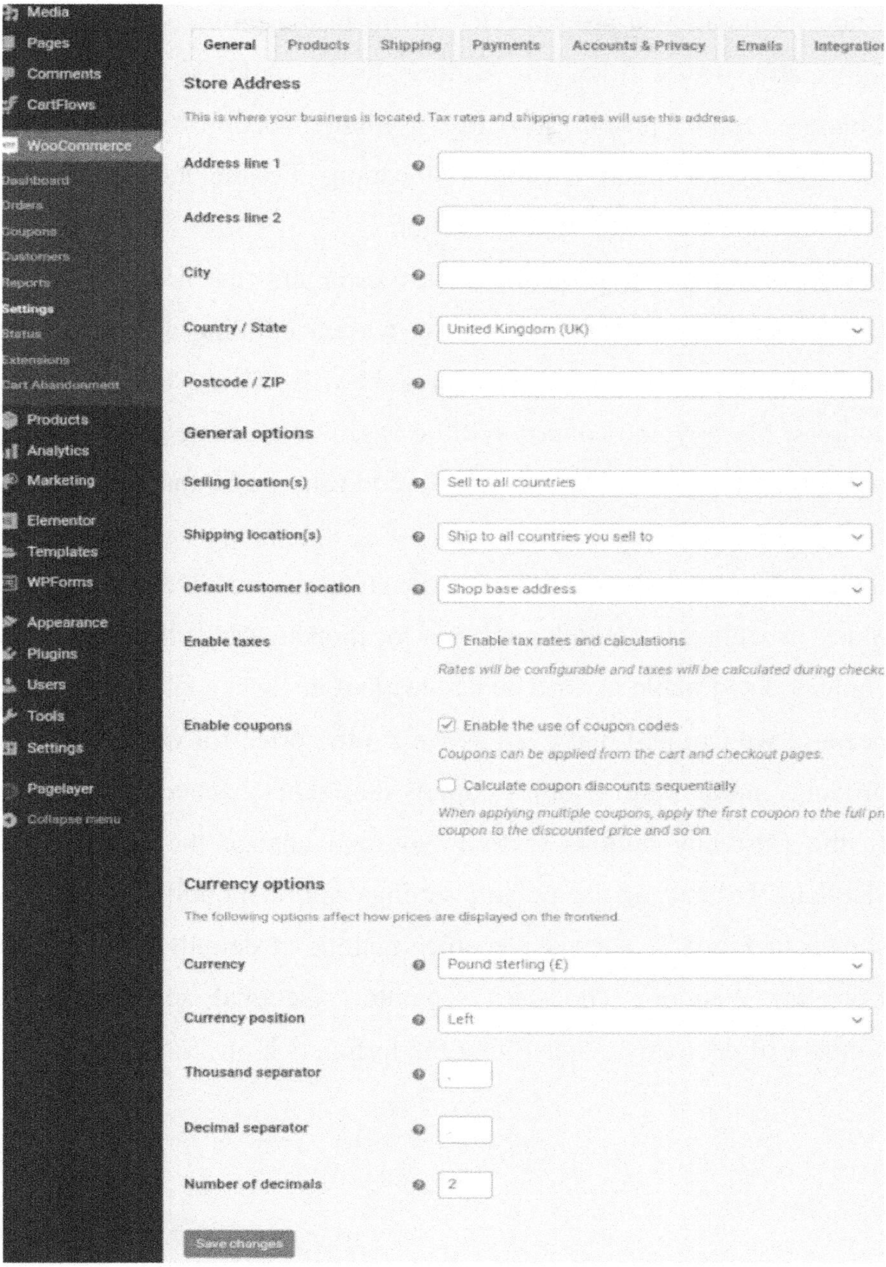

Fig 5.2: Screenshot of WooCommerce General Settings section

Under General, you are expected to fill in the provided space. The information to be filled are Address line 1, Address line 2, City, Country/ State, postal/Zip code, Selling location (s), Shipping location (s), Default customer location, Enable taxes, Enable coupons, and Currency options section.

In this teaching, we want to sell to customers that are residing in United States of America alone. So, we are building a local online store in United States. In the address, I will fill my United States address. My city and country will be based in the same country (that is United States). And my postal/Zip code should be that of a city in United States where I reside.

Selling location (s) and Shipping location should all be in United States as well. And default customer location should still be the same country. For Enable taxes, you can leave it unchecked. The reason is because we can add that even as we set the price for our individual products in our store. Enable coupons should be checked.

In the Currency options section, you can change the currency to "Dollars" instead of the default settings option Pounds Sterling as shown in Fig 5.2. Then leave other options at default settings like Currency position, Thousand separator, Decimal separator, and Number of decimals. After filling the form, click on "Save".

Store Address

This is where your business is located. Tax rates and shipping rates will use this address.

Address line 1		North Seattle
Address line 2		N/A
City		Washington
Country / State		United States (US) — Washington
Postcode / ZIP		98109

General options

Selling location(s)		Sell to specific countries
Sell to specific countries		× United States (US)
		Select all Select none
Shipping location(s)		Ship to specific countries only
Ship to specific countries		× United States (US)
		Select all Select none
Default customer location		Shop base address

Enable taxes   ☐ Enable tax rates and calculations

Rates will be configurable and taxes will be calculated during checkout.

Enable coupons   ☑ Enable the use of coupon codes

Coupons can be applied from the cart and checkout pages.

☐ Calculate coupon discounts sequentially

When applying multiple coupons, apply the first coupon to the full price coupon to the discounted price and so on.

Currency options

The following options affect how prices are displayed on the frontend.

Currency		United States (US) dollar ($)
Currency position		Left
Thousand separator		,
Decimal separator		
Number of decimals		2

[Save changes]   ⬅

Fig 5.3: Sample of my filled information in the general heading which after I am to click on Save Changes as shown by the arrow.

Products heading in Settings explains or keeps information on products you display on your e-commerce site will appear. In fact, it is the product settings of your store with WooCommerce.

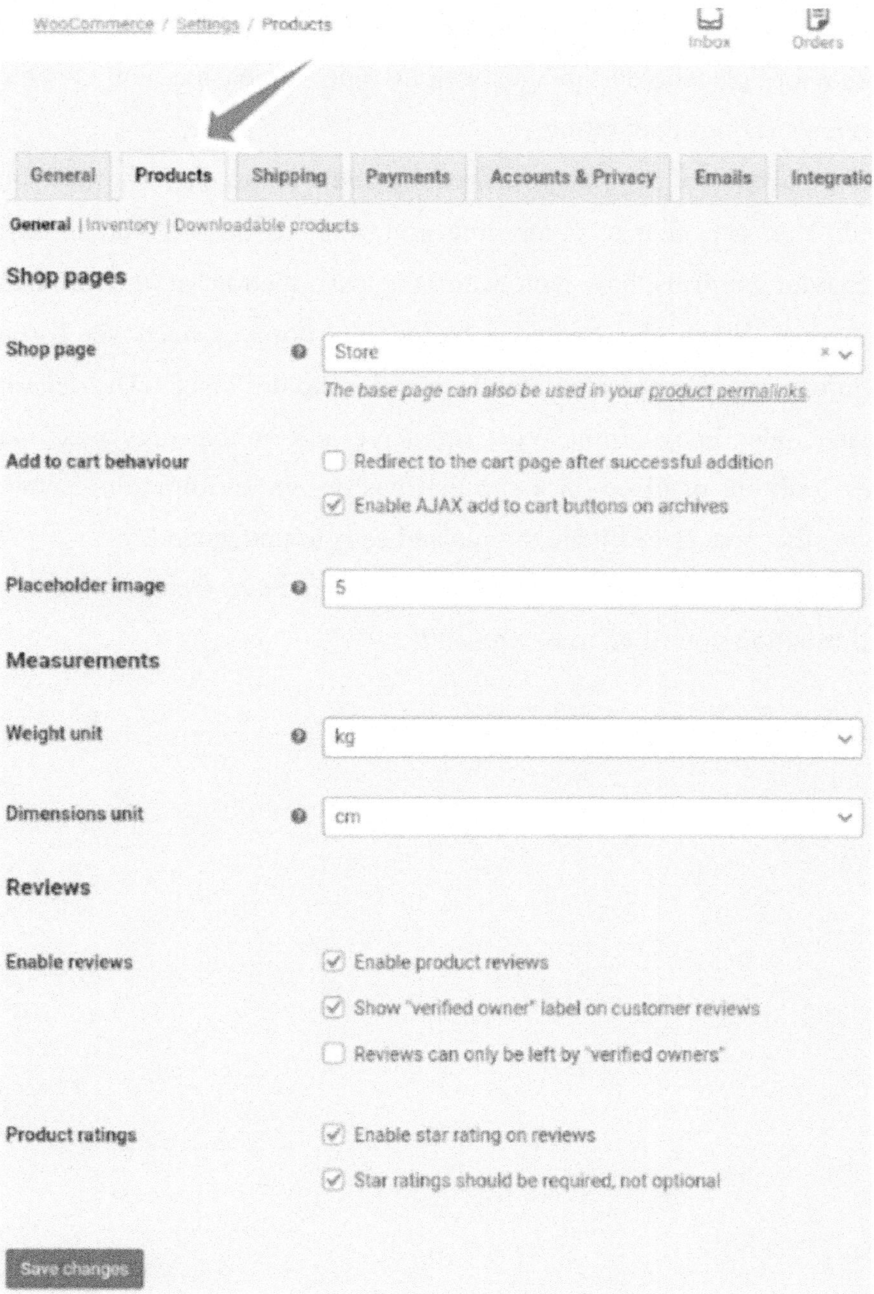

| General | **Products** | Shipping | Payments | Accounts & Privacy | Emails | Integratio |

General | Inventory | Downloadable products

Shop pages

Shop page   ❷   Store   × ∨

The base page can also be used in your product permalinks.

Add to cart behaviour   ☐ Redirect to the cart page after successful addition

                                    ☑ Enable AJAX add to cart buttons on archives

Placeholder image   ❷   5

Measurements

Weight unit   ❷   kg   ∨

Dimensions unit   ❷   cm   ∨

Reviews

Enable reviews   ☑ Enable product reviews

                                    ☑ Show "verified owner" label on customer reviews

                                    ☐ Reviews can only be left by "verified owners"

Product ratings   ☑ Enable star rating on reviews

                                    ☑ Star ratings should be required, not optional

Save changes

Fig 5.4: Screenshot of the Products heading of WooCommerce under
Settings

Where to fill in this section includes Shop page, Add to cart behavior, placeholder image, weight unit, dimension unit, enable reviews and product ratings.

Shop page is the page on your website you want to display what you sell. You can change it anytime you want to do so. Add to cart behavior controls how you want the cart section of the product function. When the Featured Image has not yet been set for a product, WooCommerce defaults to a placeholder image. The default placeholder image from WooCommerce is a simple grey box that can look out of place on a site that has design and branding setup. The other spaces to fill are simple and easy to understand.

After making changes, you are to click on Save Changes for the information you filled to be updated.

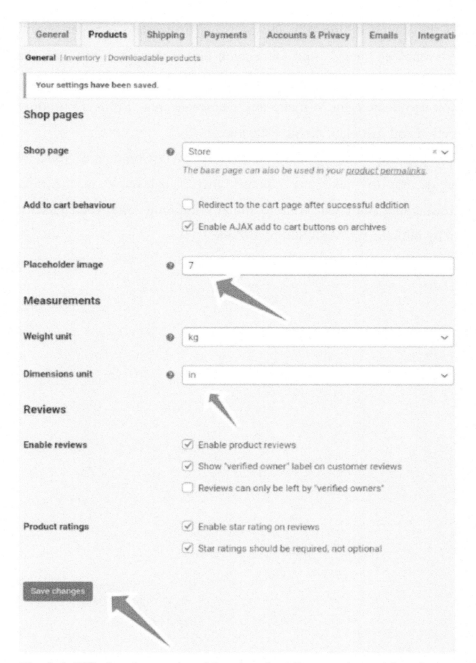

Fig 5.6: Filled and completed Product heading section with reference to "Save Changes" button

At the image of Fig 5.6, the only places I made changes are in "Placeholder image", and Dimension unit when compared with the image of Fig 5.5. And after the changes clicked on Save Changes. You can decide not to make any change in this "Product" heading section and just click on Save Changes.

For Shipping heading under Settings of WooCommerce, you can decide not to make any changes there. Just move to the next heading/tab. But if you want to add any shipping zone, you can set it up by clicking on "Add Shipping Zone".

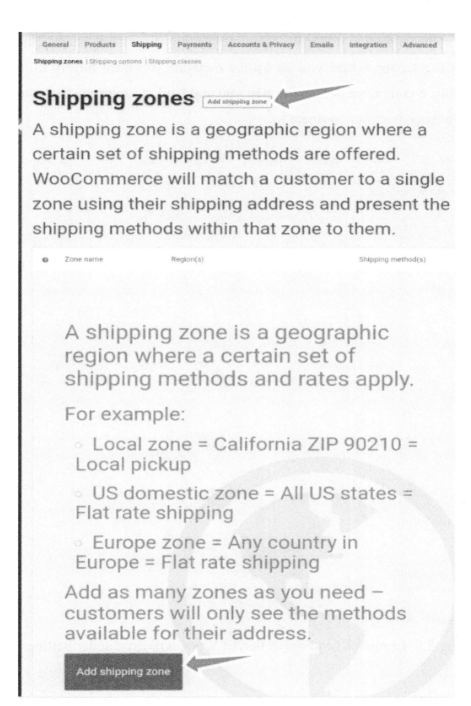

General   Products   **Shipping**   Payments   Accounts & Privacy   Emails   Integration   Advanced

Shipping zones | Shipping options | Shipping classes

Shipping zones [Add shipping zone]

A shipping zone is a geographic region where a certain set of shipping methods are offered. WooCommerce will match a customer to a single zone using their shipping address and present the shipping methods within that zone to them.

❓	Zone name	Region(s)	Shipping method(s)

A shipping zone is a geographic region where a certain set of shipping methods and rates apply.

For example:

○ Local zone = California ZIP 90210 = Local pickup

○ US domestic zone = All US states = Flat rate shipping

○ Europe zone = Any country in Europe = Flat rate shipping

Add as many zones as you need – customers will only see the methods available for their address.

[Add shipping zone]

Fig 5.7: Shipping heading section

Payments section under WooCommer setting is very important. This is the section where you set up the methods you want buyers from your e-commerce website to pay you and bank account you want to be receiving your payment to.

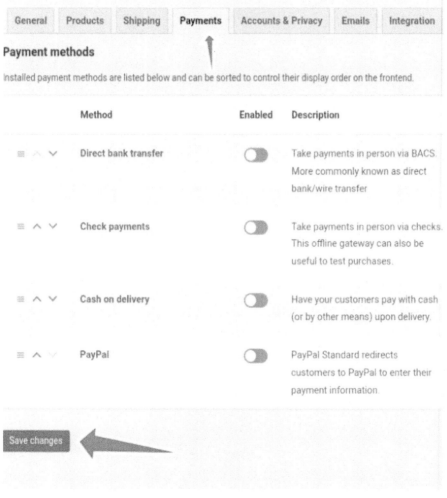

Fig 5.8: Payments heading/section of WooCommerce under Settings

The payment methods available in WooCommerce open-source commerce solution include Direct bank transfer, Check payments, Cash on delivery and PayPal. It is left for you to choose the ones you want your buyers to use and set it up. You can decide to make the four payment methods available or just few out of them.

To enable the Direct bank transfer payment method, enable it by hitting on the button-like design and it changes its color to purple.

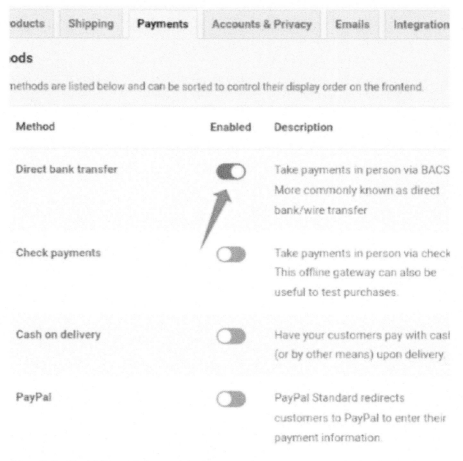

Fig 5.9: Enabling Direct bank transfer payment method as button-like design shows purple color

As the button for Direct bank transfer is enabled, click on "Manage" by the right to open a page that will give you access to add your bank account details that is in United States to receive payments from buyers.

methods are listed below and can be sorted to control their display order on the frontend.

Method	Enabled	Description	
Direct bank transfer		Take payments in person via BACS. More commonly known as direct bank/wire transfer	Manage
Check payments		Take payments in person via checks. This offline gateway can also be useful to test purchases.	Set up
Cash on delivery		Have your customers pay with cash (or by other means) upon delivery.	Set up
PayPal		PayPal Standard redirects customers to PayPal to enter their payment information.	Set up

Fig 5.1.1: Click on Manage as shown in the screenshot

When you click on Manage, another page will open. The next page that will open is shown below:

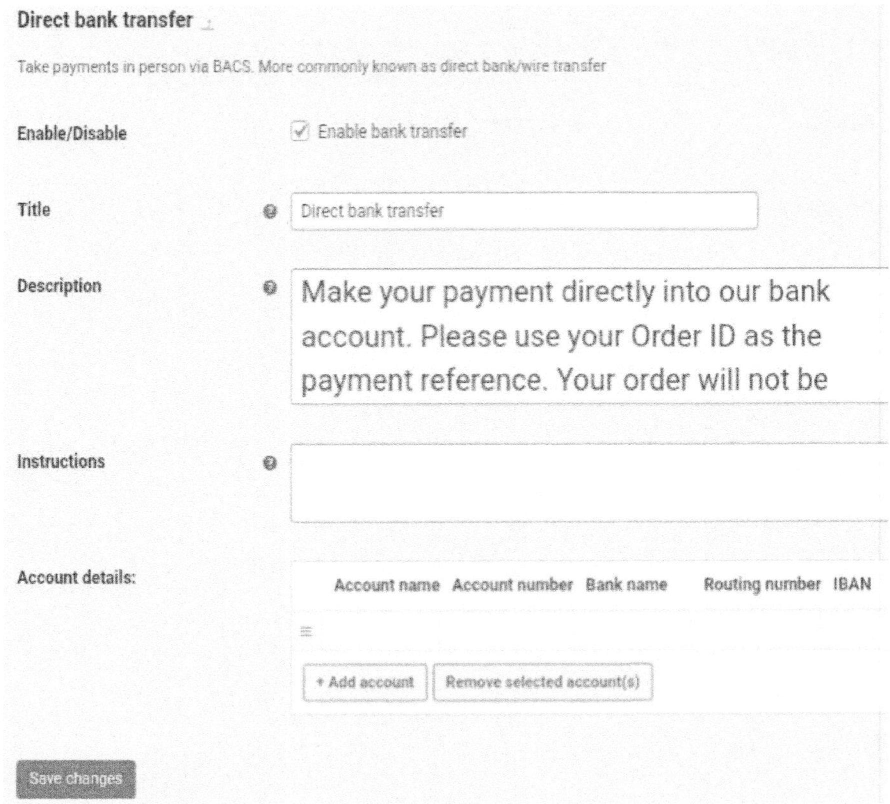

Direct bank transfer

Take payments in person via BACS. More commonly known as direct bank/wire transfer

Enable/Disable	✓ Enable bank transfer
Title	❷ Direct bank transfer
Description	❷ Make your payment directly into our bank account. Please use your Order ID as the payment reference. Your order will not be
Instructions	❷

Account details:

Account name	Account number	Bank name	Routing number	IBAN

+ Add account   Remove selected account(s)

Save changes

Fig 5.1.2: The page that opens when you click on Manage

As the page opens, in Account details section, add your Account name, Account number, Bank name, Routing number and IBAN of your bank for Europeans. The details must be that of your bank account in United States. But if you do not want to use your own bank account, you can add bank account details of anyone you want to use to receive your payment so in as much as the account is domiciled in United States. Click inside the boxes and add the details requested from you.

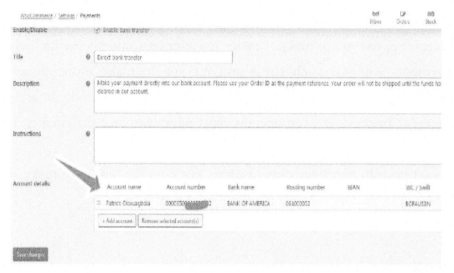

Fig 5.1.3: Filled account details section in the payments heading under the settings section of WooCommerce

Because this particular teaching section is based on setting up payment method that will sell only to buyers in United States, I do not need to fill anything in the "IBAN" because IBAN system is not applicable in United States of America.

Note: Please note that some part of the account number in Fig 5.1.3 is shaded for security purpose. You are to fill in your complete and correct account number in that space.

After you filled your bank account details correctly, click on Save Changes so that the data you entered will be saved by the system. Do not forget to click on Save Changes after filling and verifying that everything is correct.

Using PayPal Payment Method

PayPal is one of the most used payment methods in the United States. So, for you to make it easier for your customers to make their payments without much stress and for you to make more money through your e-commerce business, you have to include it as a payment method. It even accepts card payments and that makes it more interesting.

To set it up in that Payments heading, click on the button to make it enabled. In the other words to allow you to set it up.

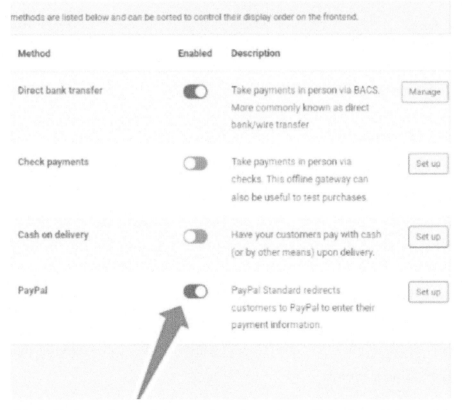

5.1.4: Button changed to purple color when clicked on it to enable set up

The next step is for you to click on Set Up by the right in the same linn with the PayPal.

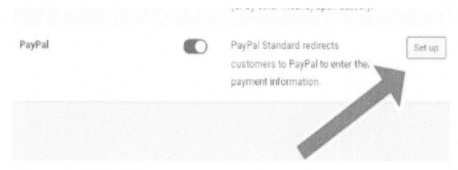

Fig 5.1.5: Click at the Set Up

When you click at Set Up, a new page opens. In that new page that opens, you may not make any remarkable changes except in a section.

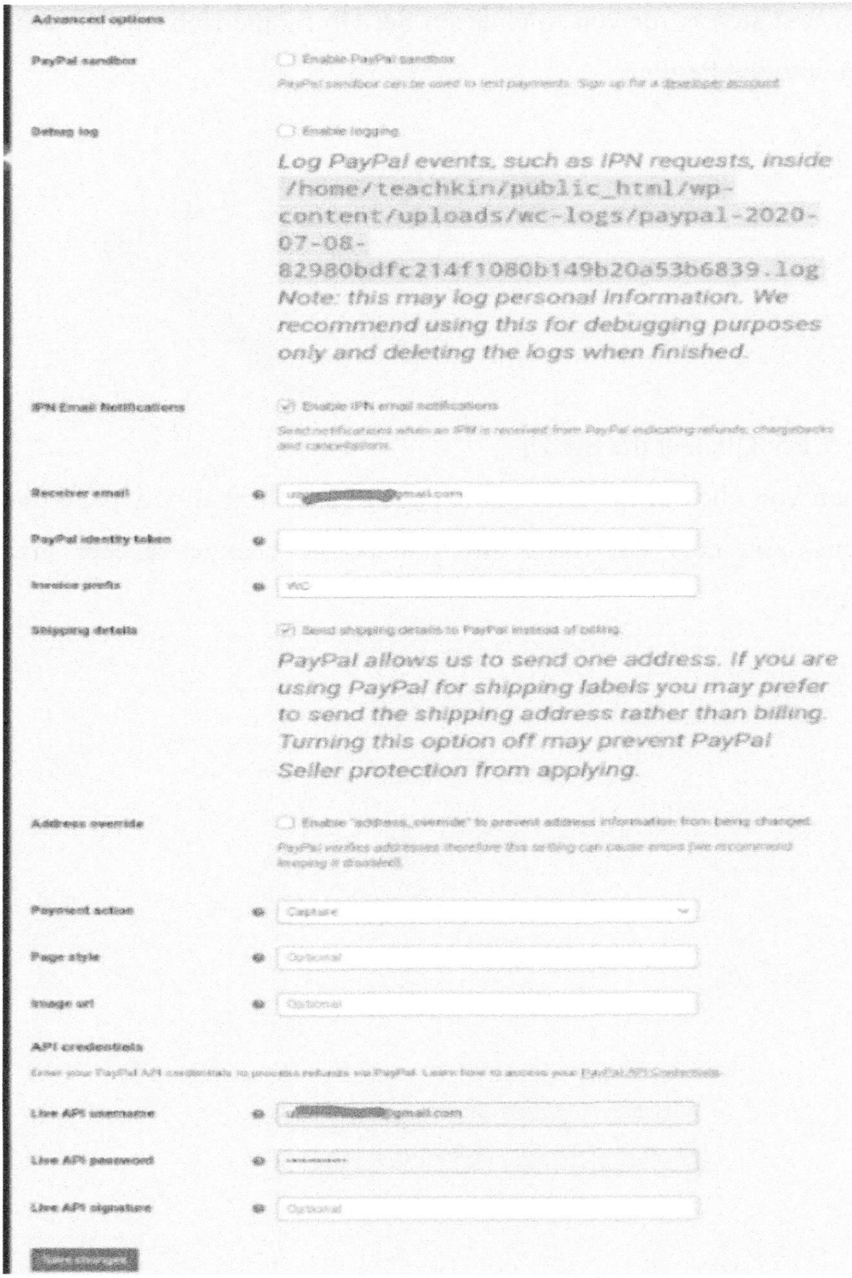

Fig 5.1.6: PayPal setup page through WooCommerce

In the Receiver email, you are to fill the email address of your PayPal business account through which you will receive payments when customers make payment using PayPal from your ecommerce website.

API credential Section in Setting up PayPal Payment Account to receive Payments

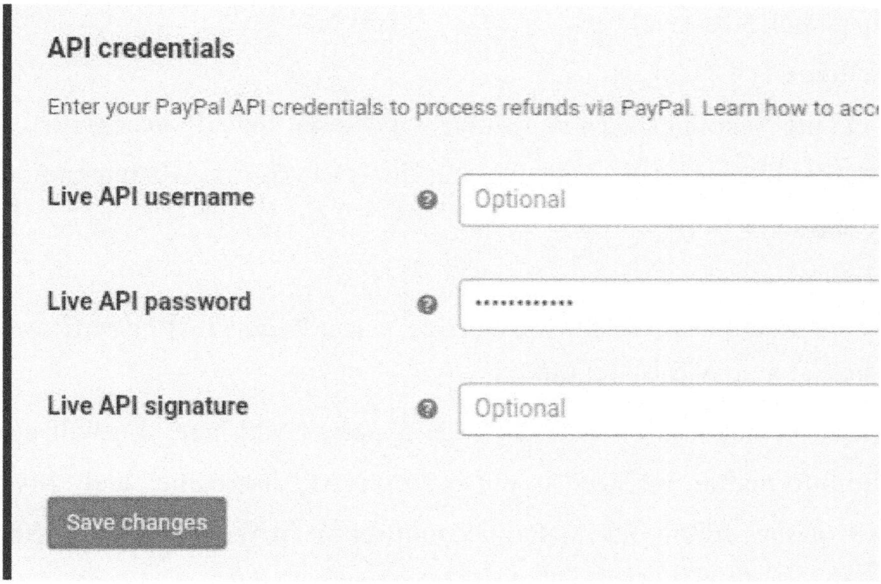

API credentials

Enter your PayPal API credentials to process refunds via PayPal. Learn how to acce

Live API username	?	Optional
Live API password	?	············
Live API signature	?	Optional

Save changes

Fig 5.1.7: The API Credentials section of PayPal set up through WooCommerce

In the above image, Fig 5.1.7, it shows the API Credentials section. You are to get "Live API username", "Live API password", and "Live API signature" which is optional. When you get this information from your PayPal business account, then you insert them in the WooCommerce PayPal payment setup section as shown in the above image.

How to create API Credentials/certificates

- For live credentials, log in to your PayPal business account at www.paypal.com or create a

new PayPal business account using the link:

https://www.paypal.com/us/merchantsignup/create

- Click the settings icon at the top of your PayPal account page and then click Account

Settings.

- On the Account access page, click Update for the API access item.

- Click Manage API Credentials in the NVP/SOAP API Integration (Classic)

section.

- On the Request API certificate page, select Request API certificate.

- Then, click Agree and Submit.

- The Manage API certificate page appears. And here you will get the information we need to put in "Live API username" and "Live API password" in out PayPal account set up in WooCommerce. So, just copy the information and paste in the space where required.

- Click Download Certificate

After inserting the required information in the WooCommerce PayPal payment Settings, just click on "Save Changes" so the data you inserted will be saved.

Fig 5.1.8: Click on Save changes to save your data

Know that the kind of PayPal account required to set up this payment method is PayPal business and not just individual PayPal account.

I believe that now you have learned how to add two payment gateways from this my teaching for stores set to make local sales only in United States of America.

First, I set up direct bank transfer payment method, and followed by PayPal payment gateway. So, if I visit the website am using to give this teaching and try to make payments of products I bought from the site, I will be given two payment options. First will be payment using bank direct deposit and the other will be payment through PayPal. You can see that in the image in Fig 5.1.9 below:

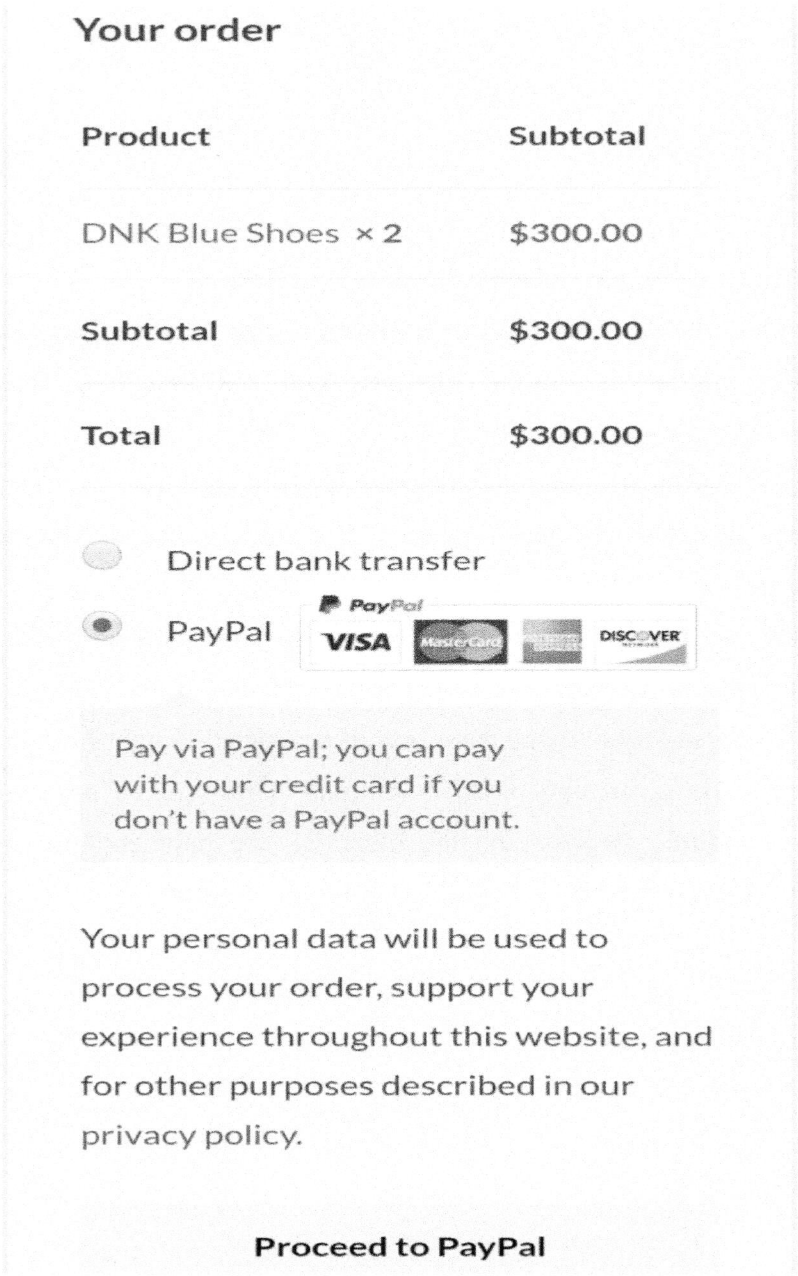

Your order

Product	Subtotal
DNK Blue Shoes × 2	$300.00
Subtotal	$300.00
Total	$300.00

○ Direct bank transfer

◉ PayPal

Pay via PayPal; you can pay with your credit card if you don't have a PayPal account.

Your personal data will be used to process your order, support your experience throughout this website, and for other purposes described in our privacy policy.

Proceed to PayPal

Fig 5.1.9: Payment methods available on the learning site.

Accounts & Privacy Heading Settings in WooCommerce

In the "Accounts & Privacy" heading under settings, please leave it as it is by default. You do not need to change anything in that Settings section.

Privacy policy

This section controls the display of your website privacy policy. The privacy notices below will not show up unless a privacy page is first set.

Personal data retention

Fig 5.2.1: Screenshot of Accounts & Privacy heading under Settings.

Emails Settings in WooCommerce

As you select Emails, in this settings heading, a new page opens. Please leave this settings option as it is. You do not necessarily need to make any change in this option unless you want to.

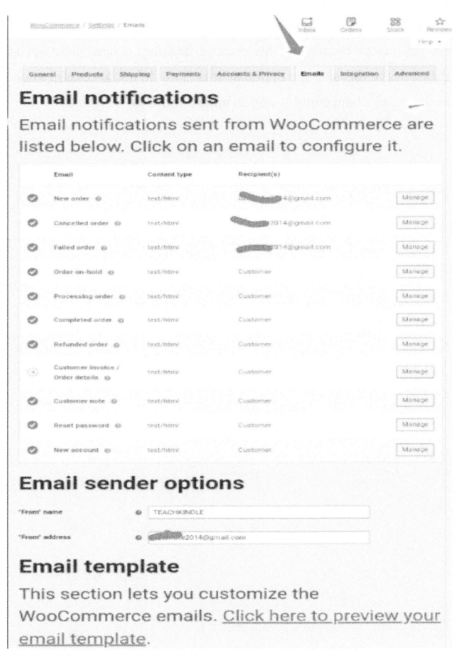

Fig 5.2.2: Email Settings of WooCommerce

Integration Settings in WooCommerce

In Integration Settings option, no remarkable change is needed, just save and proceed to the next heading.

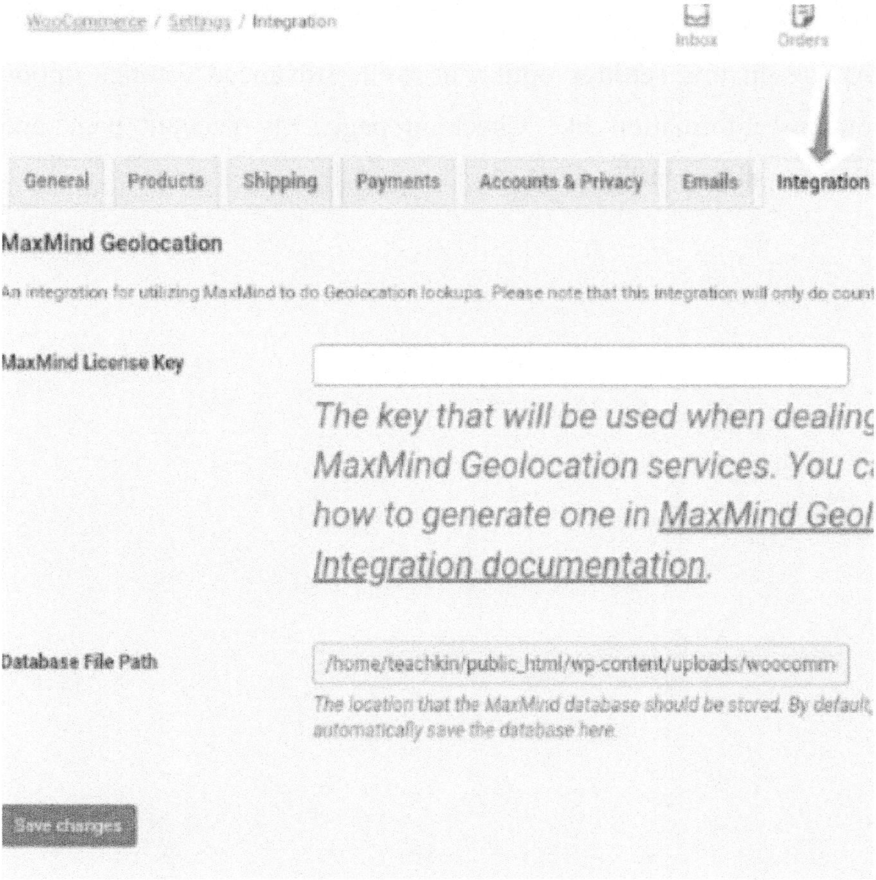

Fig 5.2.3: Integration Setting shown

Advanced Settings in WooCommerce

This settings heading shows some other further actions the administrator of the ecommerce website may feel like taking. For the sake of this teaching, you may not need to make any remarkable changes in this settings option as well. Advanced settings option contains information like Checkout page, My account page and others as shown in Fig 5.2.4.

Checkout page		Checkout	× ∨
My account page		My account	× ∨
Terms and conditions		Select a page...	∨

Checkout endpoints

Endpoints are appended to your page URLs to handle specific actions during the checkout process. They should be unique.

Pay		order-pay
Order received		order-received
Add payment method		add-payment-method
Delete payment method		delete-payment-method
Set default payment method		set-default-payment-method

Account endpoints

Endpoints are appended to your page URLs to handle specific actions on the accounts pages. They should be unique and can be left blank to disable the endpoint.

Orders		orders
View order		view-order
Downloads		downloads
Edit account		edit-account
Addresses		edit-address
Payment methods		payment-methods
Lost password		lost-password
Logout		customer-logout

Fig 5.2.4: Advanced settings option shown

Note: If you want to see the performance of your ecommerce website, click on WooCommerce and then select dashboard of the WooCommerce plugin.

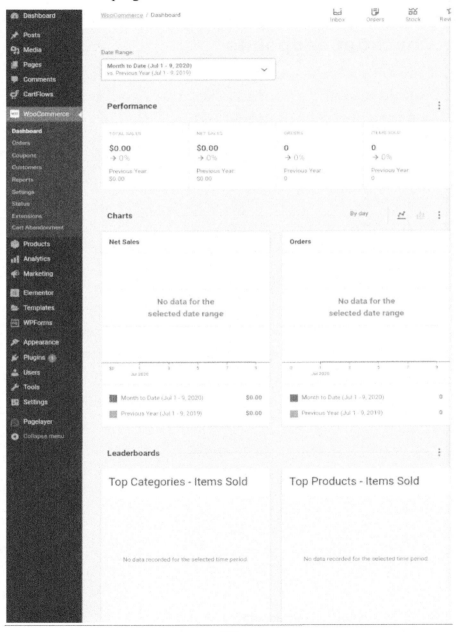

Fig 5.2.5: The dashboard of my WooCommerce plugin.

The dashboard above is without sales because I just built it for the purpose of this teaching. But for completely built ecommerce store, the site performance shows at the dashboard.

Also, if you want to see the number of orders you have received from people, just click on Orders. You can play around the other options under WooCommercer and see what they have to offer.

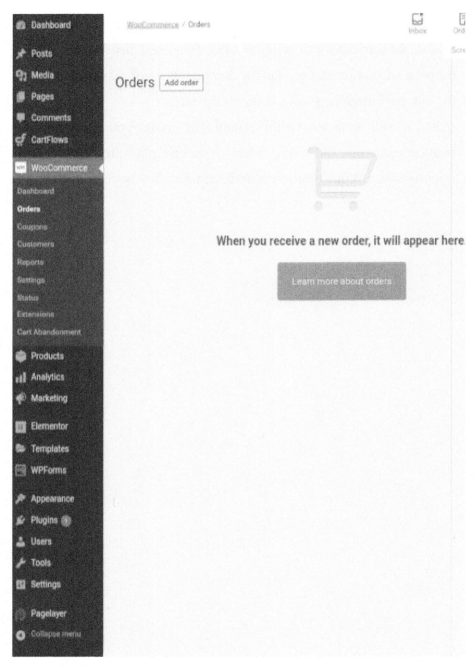

Fig 5.2.6: Screenshot shows the "Orders" section of WooCommerce

Setting up Payment Gateway for Ecommerce Websites in India

India as a country has population of approximately 1.353 billion in 2018 record according to World Bank report. India is an Asia country that is growing speedily in tech in the recent time. The country is also going deep in e-commerce website building. It is an area of interest and that is why I decided to create this subheading so that e-commerce website builders from India can learn how to set up payment gateway for their websites. It is a target country for international e-commerce business companies. That is why Amazon targets the country among other Asian countries.

In this subheading, I assume that I want to build an ecommerce website that I want to use to sell products locally in India. The buyers I am accepting in this my online store is only buyers from India as well. I am not accepting buyers from outside India in this teaching.

The steps in setting up my account in this teaching is not far from how I did it when I taught you how to build an ecommerce store in United States. Note that am going to remove the setup I made during my teaching on building an ecommerce website in United States of America in other to set a new country of target as India. But not to worry too much because I will take you on step by step guide on how to achieve this task.

I will be choosing a different payment gateway different from PayPal here. The payment gateway I will be teaching you with to receive payment from buyers is the one called Instamojo.

Instamojo is one of the top-rated payment gateway & e-commerce platform in India. It is trusted by 1200000+ Indian small businesses. Instamojo is India's largest on-demand payments and ecommerce platform that empowers over 1,200,000 micro-entrepreneurs, startups, MSMEs, to start, manage, and grow their business online across mobile and web, with just a bank account and phone number, in a few minutes. The company has many positive reviews on the services they render to e-commerce website builders.

Because I will be using Instamojo payment gateway in my ecommerce website, I have to first install the Instamojo plugin in my WordPress. It is from there that I will then set it up as a payment gateway for my website.

How to Install Instamojo Plugin on WordPress.

To install Instamojo payment gateway plugin, follow the following steps:

- Login to your WordPress dashboard or select dashboard if you are already logged in

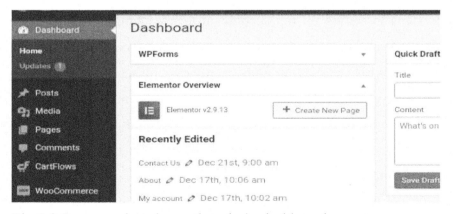

Fig 5.2.7: screenshot shows the admin dashboard

- Select Plugins

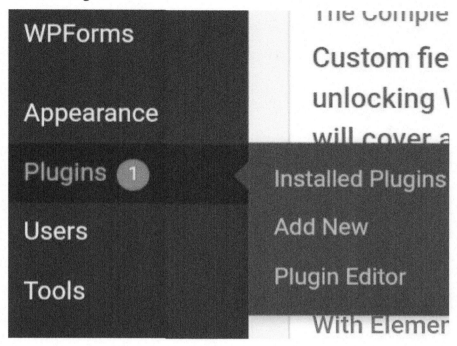

Fig 5.2.8: Plugin screen option shown

- Select Add New

- Type Instamojo for WooCommerce in the provided search box

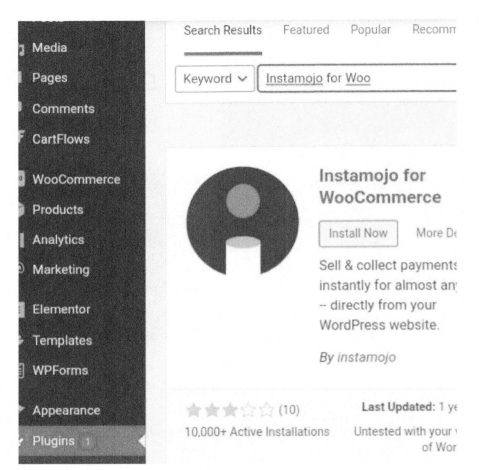

Fig 5.2.9: Screenshot as Instamojo for WooCommerce is typed into the plugins search box

- Select the plugin (the Instamojo)
- Click on Install Now
- Click on Activate

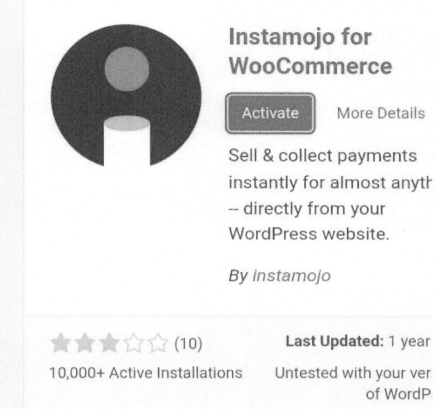

Fig 5.3.1: Image shows Activate button to click

With this last step, you have Instamojo as one of your active plugins waiting to be setup.

Practical: Setting up the Instamojo for WooCommerce

Here, I will be teaching you how to set up Instamojo for WooCommerce for your online store in India for you to be able to receive payments from buyers. To do that, adhere to the following guide:

- Select Plugins among the WordPress screen options

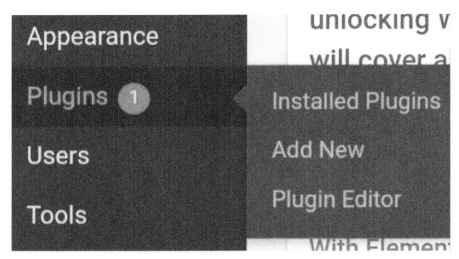

Fig 5.3.2: Select Plugins as shown on the image

- Select Installed plugins

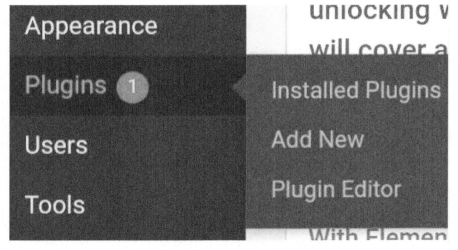

Fig 5.3.3: Select Installed Plugins which is the first option when Plugins is Selected

- Search in the list of installed plugins and you will see Instamojo for WooCommerce

- Click on the Settings of Instamojo for WooCommerce

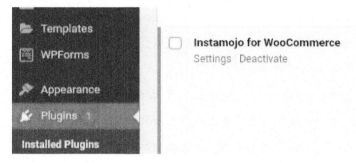

Fig 5.3.4: Select Settings which appears under the "Instamojo for WooCommerce"

- Fill the information required of you

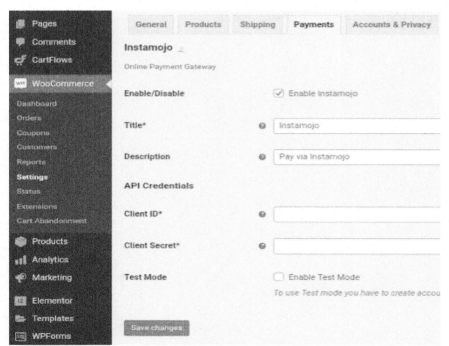

Fig 5.3.5: The new page that opens when Settings is clicked on

In Fig 5.3.5, you are to fill in that form. In the API Credentials section, we are to get the Client ID and Client Secret from Instamojo website.

How to get API Credentials Information from Instamojo to setup Payments Method with WooCommerce

To get these data, follow the listed guide below:

- Open a new tab in your browser

This will make you not to be logged out of WordPress platform. It will make it easy for you to copy the API Credentials you need and then visit the tab you were working on before to paste the needed information.

- Type in www.instamojo.com in the new browser tab and then search

- Select Signup as the website opens

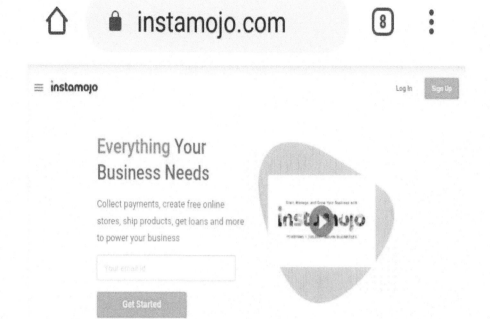

Fig 5.3.6: The landing page of Instamojo website with "Sign Up" at the top right-hand side

- Fill the information required from you

When a new page opens when you Select Signup, please select business before filling other few information required from you.

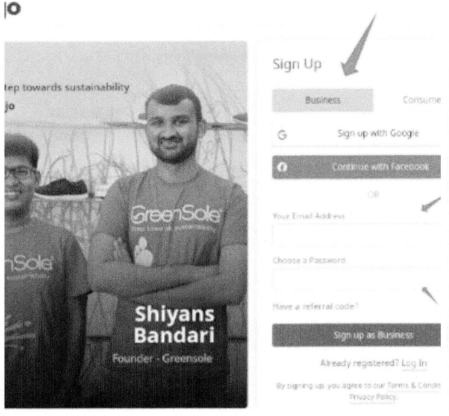

Fig 5.3.7: Selecting Business account and filling the required information

- Click Sign Up as Business

When you finish filling the information demanded from you for the sign up, you click on Sign Up as Business for your account to be registered.

- Insert your Indian phone number for verification

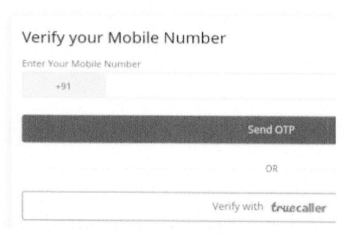

Fig 5.3.8: Insert your Indian phone number to receive OTP

As you insert your Indian phone number, One Time Password (OTP) will be sent to it. Insert the OTP to the space provided for you. Once the verification is done, then you have full access to the payment gateway after few other steps.

- Choose the option (1) that describes whether you run the business yourself as an individual, or whether it is a registered organization like a LLP, Private Limited, NGO etc. Choose the appropriate option in (2) and click Next (3) to Continue as shown below:

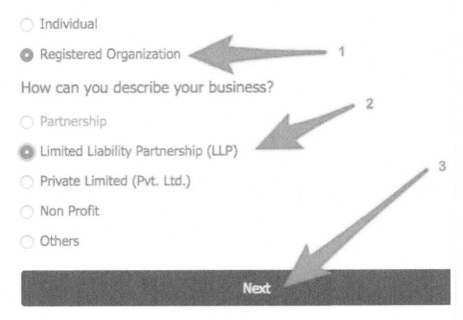

What type of Business are you?

○ Individual

◉ Registered Organization ← ─── 1

How can you describe your business?

○ Partnership

◉ Limited Liability Partnership (LLP) ← 2

○ Private Limited (Pvt. Ltd.) 3

○ Non Profit

○ Others

Next

Fig 5.3.9: Choosing the type of business you run

- Enter your/business PAN number and your/business name as it appears on the PAN card (1). Enter your/business address, state and pin code (2). If applicable to your business, enter the GSTIN (3). Finally, select the appropriate option that applies to your business in (4) and click Next (5). This is as described in the image below:

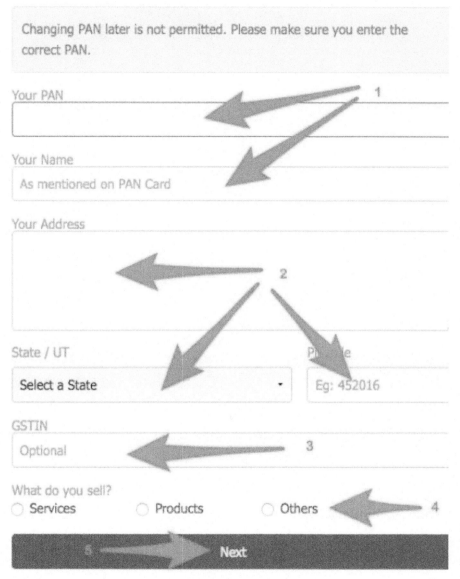

Fig 5.4.1: Filling of government mandatory details with Instamojo - Choose a username that matches your business (1) or pick a suggested username if you like (2) and click on Next (3) to continue.

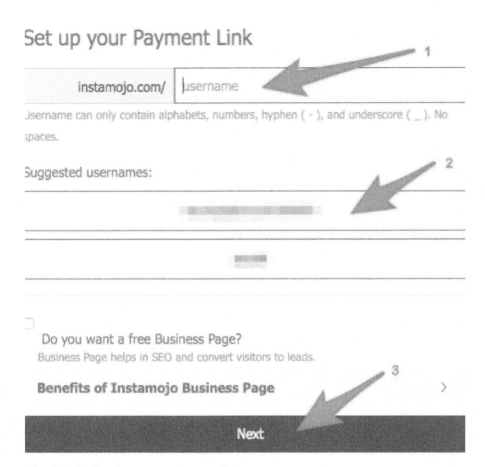

Fig 5.4.2: Setting up payment link

- You are almost done! Enter your bank account number (1) and IFSC code (3) to receive payouts. Confirm that the account name (2) matches with the bank's records. Finally click on Accept Terms and Create Account (4).

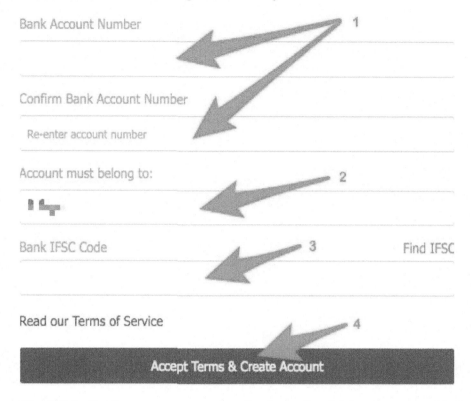

Fig 5.4.3: Setting up account details through which you get paid to your bank account

After this stage, you will be logged in to your Instamojo account dashboard. So, the next thing is to get you API Credentials information which is what we need to link the Instamojo account with WooCommerce.

- Click on API and Plugins section

Since you are already at the dashboard section of your Instamojo account, click on API & Plugins which is shown on the image below:

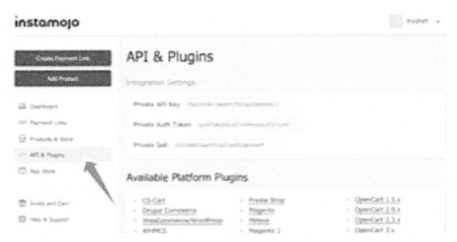

Fig 4.4.4: The position of API & Plugins shown on Instamojo account

- Click on Create new Credentials

Fig 4.4.5: Position of Create new Credentials shown

- Select the Platform/Framework from the dropdown for which you want to generate Client ID and Client Secret, and from that dropdown, Select WooCommerce/WordPress

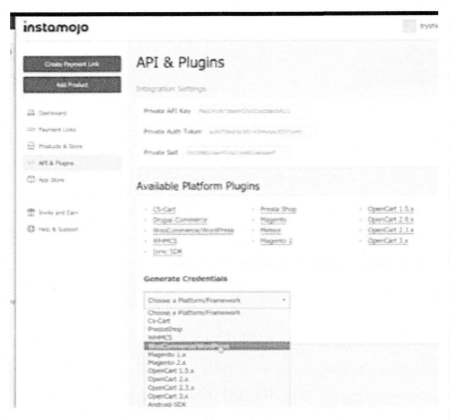

Fig 4.4.6: Selecting WooCommerce/WordPress as platform to use API Credentials

- Click Generate Credentials

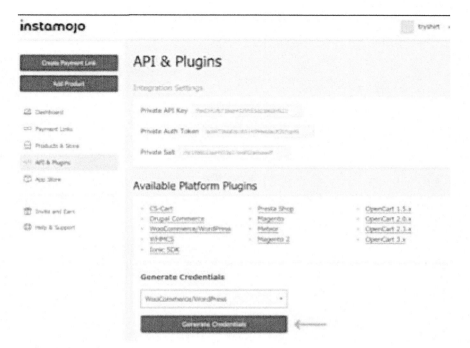

Fig 4.4.7: Clicking on Generate Credentials

When you click Generate Credentials, your Client ID and Client Secret will display.

Fig 4.4.8: The screenshot of the generated Client ID and Client Secret

Placing the API Credentials in your Instamojo for WooCommerce plugin

Go back to your WordPress platform. Then in the Plugins, click on Installed Plugins, and then look for Instamojo for WooCommerce, click on the settings. This was where I stopped in the previous teaching before I dived into "How to get API Credentials Information from Instamojo to set up Payments Method with WooCommerce"

So, fill in the "API Client ID" and "API Secret" obtained from Instamojo account in the two spaces.

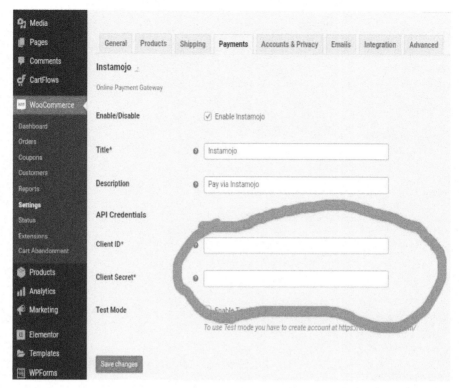

Fig 5.4.9: Where to fill in the generated Client ID and Client Secret

- Then click on Save Changes

Setting up your ECommerce Location to India and Targeting only Indian Buyers

To achieve this task, click on "General" in the Settings of WooCommerce page which where you are currently.

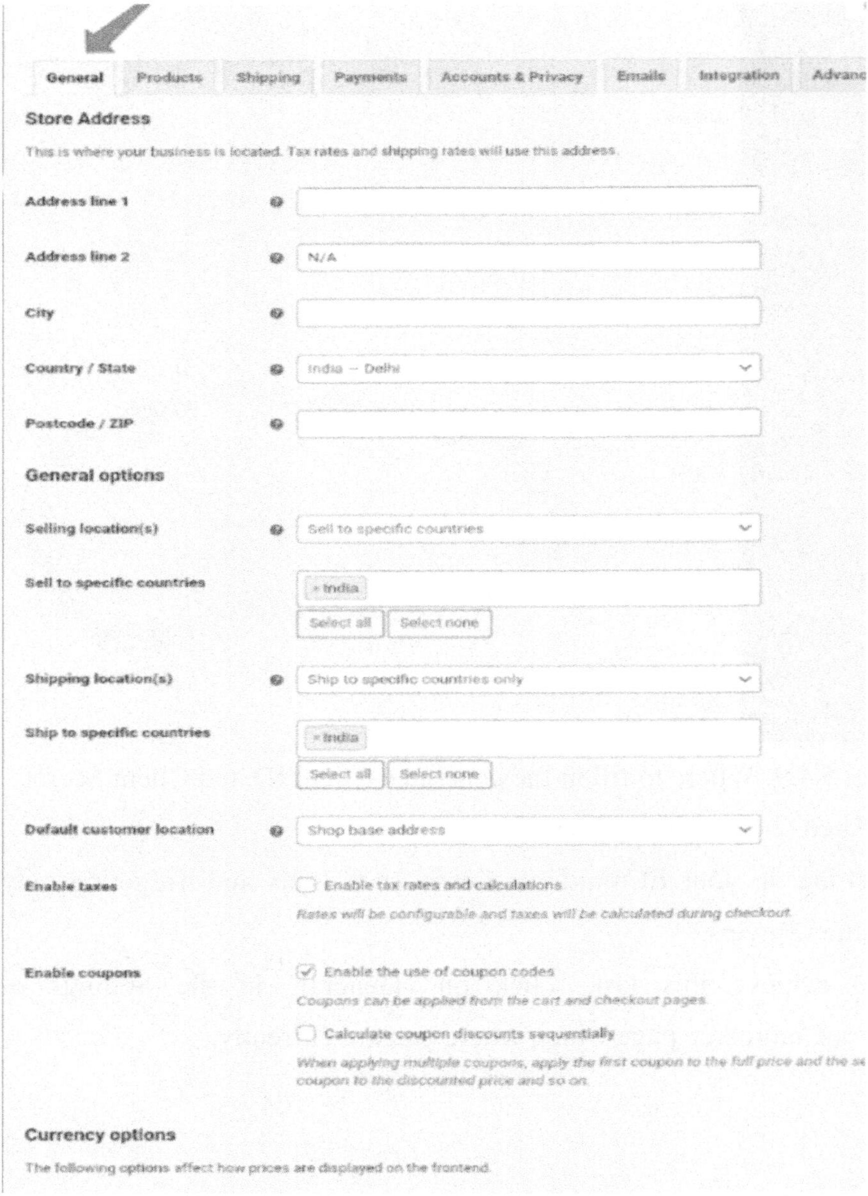

General   Products   Shipping   Payments   Accounts & Privacy   Emails   Integration   Advanc

Store Address

This is where your business is located. Tax rates and shipping rates will use this address.

Address line 1

Address line 2   N/A

City

Country / State   India — Delhi

Postcode / ZIP

General options

Selling location(s)   Sell to specific countries

Sell to specific countries   × India

Select all   Select none

Shipping location(s)   Ship to specific countries only

Ship to specific countries   × India

Select all   Select none

Default customer location   Shop base address

Enable taxes   ☐ Enable tax rates and calculations

Rates will be configurable and taxes will be calculated during checkout.

Enable coupons   ☑ Enable the use of coupon codes

Coupons can be applied from the cart and checkout pages.

☐ Calculate coupon discounts sequentially

When applying multiple coupons, apply the first coupon to the full price and the se
coupon to the discounted price and so on.

Currency options

The following options affect how prices are displayed on the frontend.

Fig 4.5.1: Complete the information under the general settings with
Indian details

Set all information to be dirctected to India. So, your target buyers are only Indians. After this, click on "Save Changes"

Chapter 6

Setting up Payment Gateways for Ecommerce Stores in African Countries

Africa is coming up in e-commerce website building. In the recent time, there are many e-commerce websites in African countries. That is the reason I decided to give this section a different chapter heading.

African is not known to be a place where technology is highly amplified. But because of the growth in online stores in that location, I decided to teach on how to set up payment gateways for targeted customers that want to buy in that location. I am focusing on payment gateways because that is the main thing. If customers are interested in the products you sell in your online stores but cannot make payment, that is rubbish. So, I am here to teach you how you can set that up.

For other areas like adding products to your websites and design of the website, it is the same irrespective of your location. So, you can learn that from my written chapters and other chapters to read. I am focusing on payments in African countries because it is specific to the location.

If you are an American, it is possible to be contacted by a business company in any African country to build e-commerce website for them to use to drive market in the country. They may want the website to target only buyers from the country which this chapter is focusing on. The question is, how can you set up payment gateways in that location? How can you make it work? By the end of this chapter, the above question will be answered. It is a step by step guide for you to get the task completed.

According to the UNCTAD E-commerce Index Report 2018, Nigeria, South Africa and Kenya account for more than half of the online shoppers in Africa in 2017. Nigeria is Africa's largest business to consumer e-commerce market in terms of both number of shoppers and revenue.

With the above record, I will be using Nigeria as an African country to carry out the teaching on how to set up payment gateways for an e-commerce website/store in Africa. As earlier said, I will be targeting local buyers in Nigeria. So, the e-commerce website will not ship to any country outside Nigeria.

There are payment gateways that work effective in Nigeria, among them is WooCommerce, FirstPay Link, PayStack and Remita.

This chapter is important because there are many young people from African countries that are fast growing in Tech. Some of them want to learn how to build e-commerce websites and set up payment gateways for receiving payments but find it difficult to lay their hands on materials that will teach them how to do so. This is a sound material to help them learn the skill.

This chapter is so detailed in a way that someone who does not know anything on setting up payment gateways in African countries before can know how to get the job done after reading this. I am here for you. I am your teacher in this area and do not hesitate to write to me through my email if you have any difficulty as you go on with your work in building e-commerce payment gateway in any country in Africa which this chapter is addressing. My email address is on one of the last chapters of this book.

List of Payment Gateways Acceptable on E-commerce Websites in Africa

If you are building an e-commerce website for clients in Africa, these are among the payment gateways acceptable in the Continent that you can use to build the online stores:

- PayU
- PayStack
- Paygate
- Flutterwave
- GTPay
- Pesapal
- Interswitch Webpay
- eTtranzact
- 2Checkout
- VoguePay
- Wirecard
- SimplePay

- CashEnvoy

- Coinbase Commerce

- FirstPay Link

- GlobalPay

- PayU

- PayFast

- U-Collect

- PayPal Express Checkout

- DusuPay

- BitPay

- Remita and

- Peach Payments

Apart from all these listed payment gateways, you can use Google to search for reliable payment gateways that work well in a specific country in Africa. It will help you build with sound payment gateways for your clients from any part of Africa.

Step by Step Guide in Setting up Payment Gateway on E-commerce Website in Nigeria

The first thing is to decide on a payment gateway you want to make use of. This gateway will help you accept payments from buyers and then remit to your bank account you will registered with them. So, if you get contracted by someone in Nigeria to build an e-commerce store for him, you have many payment gateways to choose from.

In this teaching, I am using a payment gateway called Remita to build my e-commerce website targeted at Nigerian buyers only and located in Nigeria. So, I will fill all the information needed in this teaching in respect to Nigeria as my marketplace. The merchant am building this website for in this teaching does not need international buyers. Everything centers in that African country.

Even though am using Remita as the payment gateway in this teaching, other reliable payment gateways to be used in Nigeria for e-commerce websites building are FirstPay Link and PayStack. Fast emerging as Africa's preferred payment platform, Remita is chosen by millions of people and thousands of organizations. It is the default payment gateway that facilitates the Federal Government of Nigeria's Treasury Single Account (TSA), the largest and most impactful of its kind in Africa. Remita launched in 2005 and is fully developed in Lagos Nigeria by SystemSpecs.

Account Creation with Remita Payment Gateway

To create account with Remita which you need to aid you get paid, do the following:

- Visit the website at www.remita.net

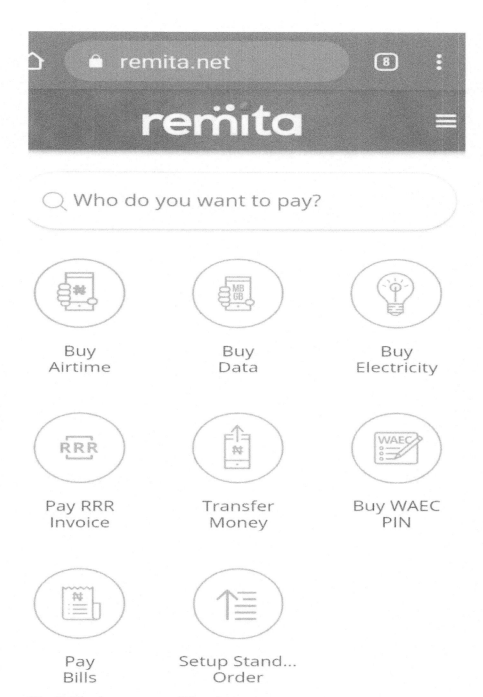

Fig 6: The homepage of Remita payment gateway

- Select the website menu bar

Fig 6.1: Arrow points at the menu bar

- Under the Integration menu item, select "-Become an Integrator"

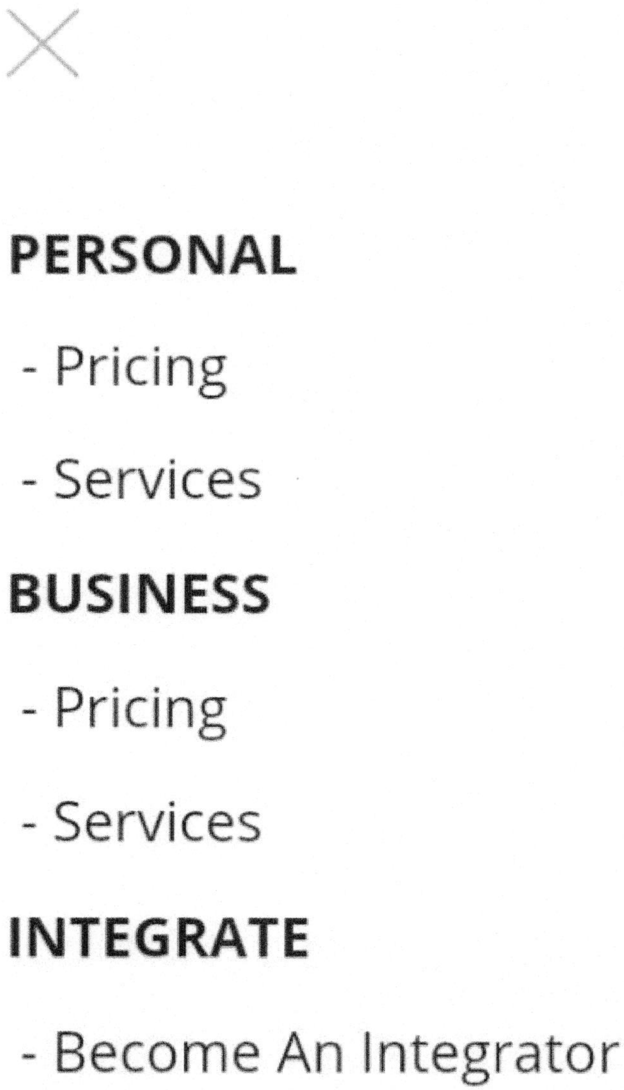

PERSONAL

- Pricing

- Services

BUSINESS

- Pricing

- Services

INTEGRATE

- Become An Integrator

Fig 6.2: Select -Become an Integrator as shown in the image
- Scroll down and select "Get Started"

GO LIVE

Fig 6.3: Select Get Started

- Fill the required information in the form

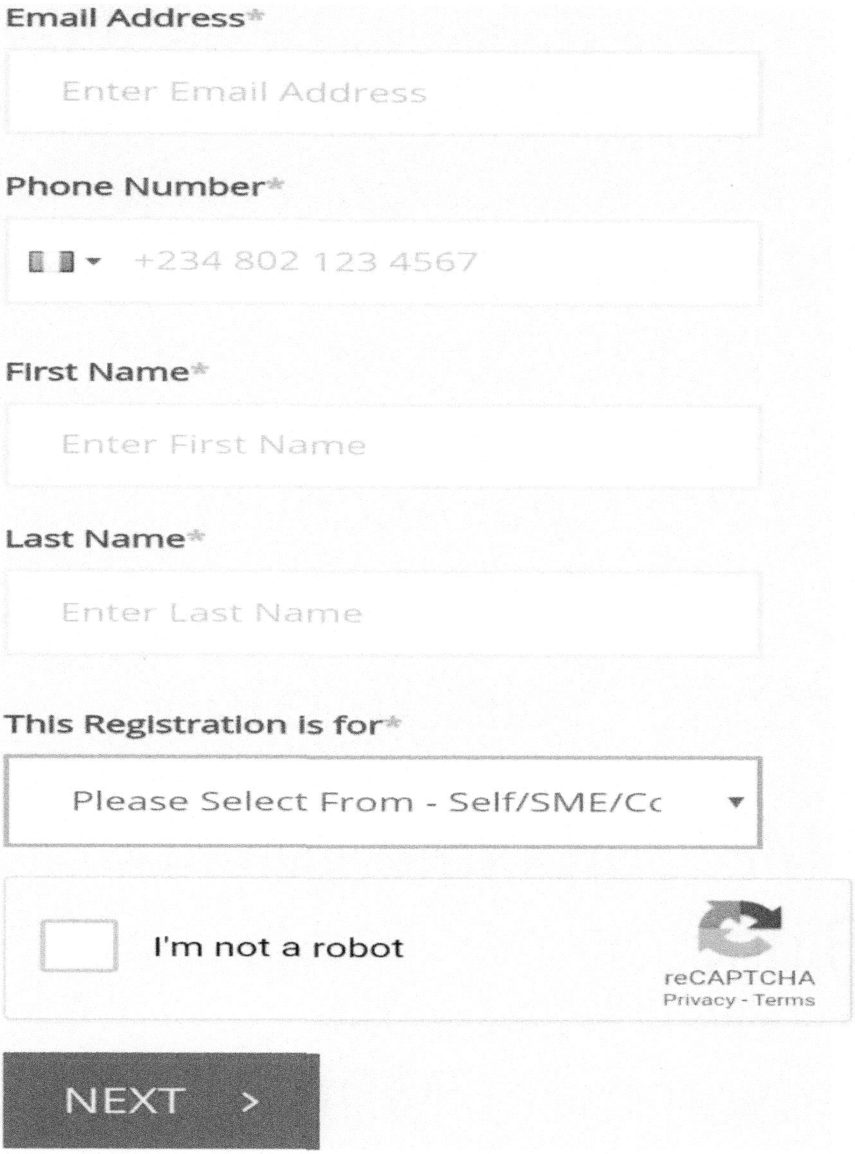

Email Address*

> Enter Email Address

Phone Number*

> ▮ ▮ ▼   +234 802 123 4567

First Name*

> Enter First Name

Last Name*

> Enter Last Name

This Registration is for*

> Please Select From - Self/SME/Cc   ▼

☐ I'm not a robot	reCAPTCHA Privacy - Terms

NEXT >

Fig 6.4: Fill the information required in the form

- Tick "I'm not a robot" reCAPTCHA if it appears
- Click "Next" to continue with your registration

- Select from the dropdown what the registration is for.

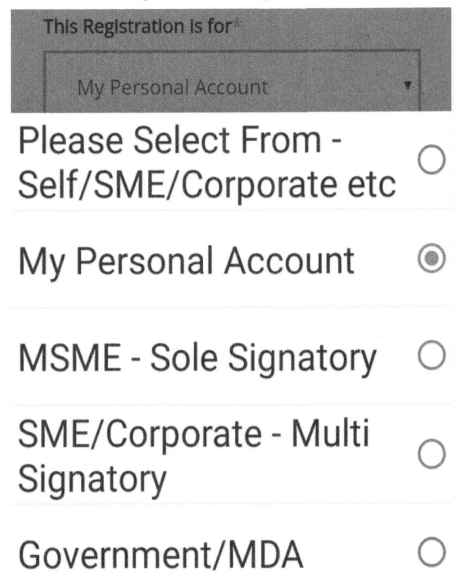

Fig 6.5: Selecting from the dropdown what the registration is for

If you are registration is for private or personal business, tick "My Personal Account"

- Then click "Next" and One Time Password (OTP) will be sent to the phone number you entered
- Type the OTP in the space provided for you on the site for verification and then click on "Next"

A Verification Code Has Been Sent To Your Phone

Please enter OTP

Fig 6.6: Type in the OTP in the box

- Once the entered OTP is correct, you will see a notification on your device screen advising you to login to your email to continue with your registration.

An email has been sent to you to complete the registration process

Fig 6.7: The notification you will see when an email is sent to you

- Login to the email address you filled with Remita, open the mail sent by the company, and click on the hyperlinked phrase containing the link you are advised to click on to complete your registration

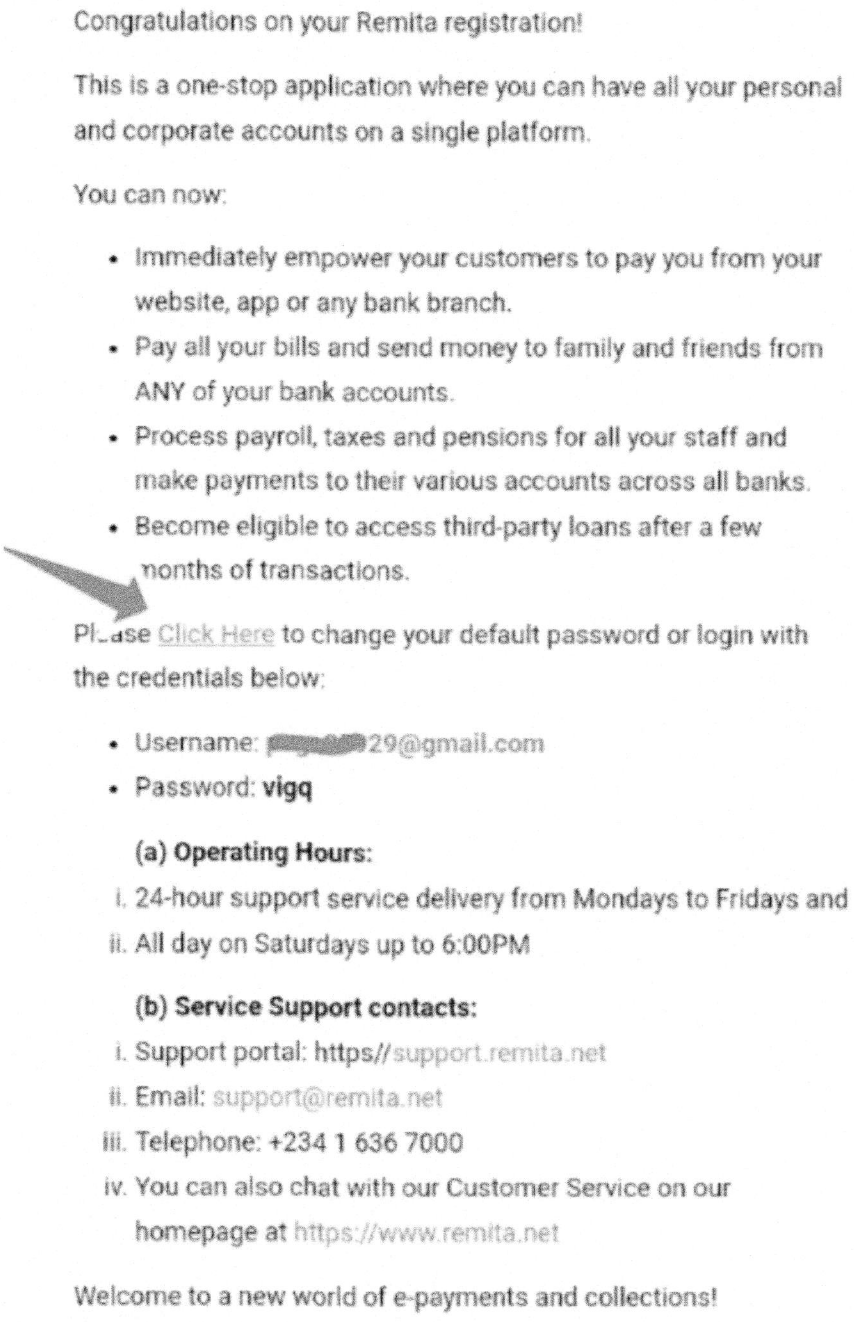

Congratulations on your Remita registration!

This is a one-stop application where you can have all your personal and corporate accounts on a single platform.

You can now:

- Immediately empower your customers to pay you from your website, app or any bank branch.
- Pay all your bills and send money to family and friends from ANY of your bank accounts.
- Process payroll, taxes and pensions for all your staff and make payments to their various accounts across all banks.
- Become eligible to access third-party loans after a few months of transactions.

Please Click Here to change your default password or login with the credentials below:

- Username: ~~████~~29@gmail.com
- Password: **vigq**

(a) Operating Hours:

i. 24-hour support service delivery from Mondays to Fridays and

ii. All day on Saturdays up to 6:00PM

(b) Service Support contacts:

i. Support portal: https//support.remita.net

ii. Email: support@remita.net

iii. Telephone: +234 1 636 7000

iv. You can also chat with our Customer Service on our homepage at https://www.remita.net

Welcome to a new world of e-payments and collections!

Fig 6.8: Example of e-mail and where to click on

- Change your password

As you click on the link, it opens in a new browser tab requesting you create a new password. Create the new password and then click on "Set Next Password".

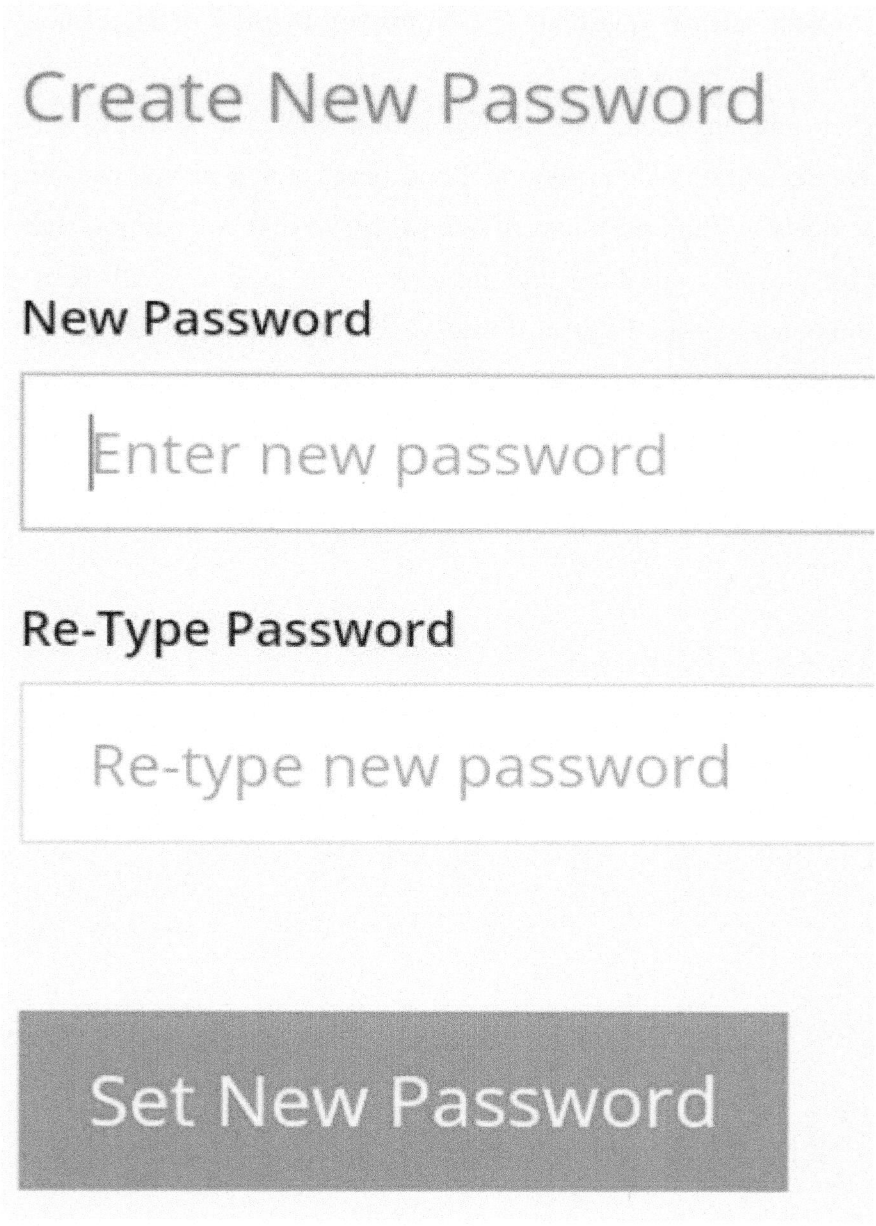

Create New Password

New Password

Enter new password

Re-Type Password

Re-type new password

Set New Password

Fig 6.9: Enter your new password and save

- Answer security questions chosen for you by the system or choose for yourself and answer.

After you answered the two questions, click on "Set Answers". Security questions are important and because of that you can write the questions and the answers somewhere so that you can remember them. Security questions and answers can be used to verify your e-commerce website in case of loss of account or when security issue is detected on your account.

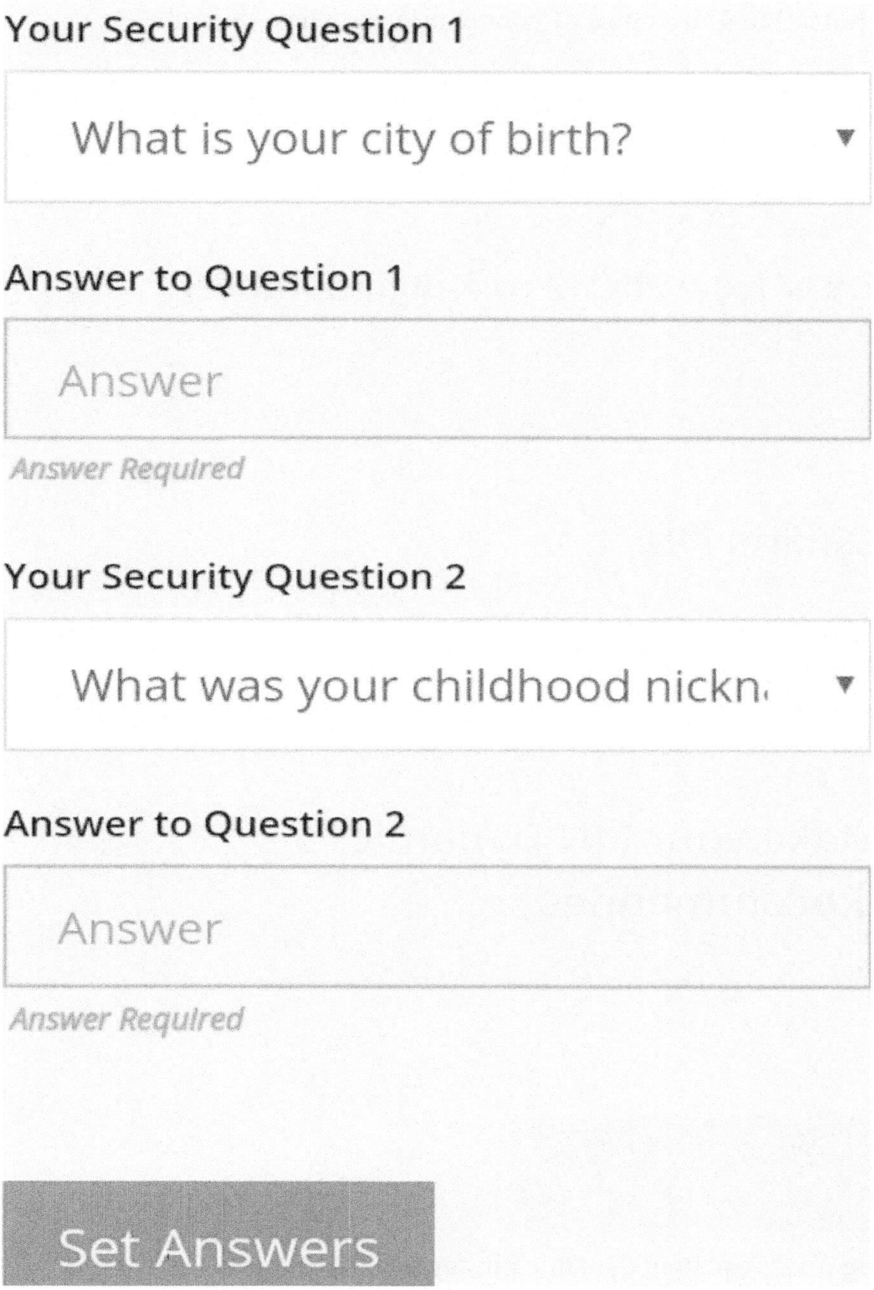

Your Security Question 1

What is your city of birth? ▼

Answer to Question 1

Answer

Answer Required

Your Security Question 2

What was your childhood nickn. ▼

Answer to Question 2

Answer

Answer Required

Set Answers

Fig 6.1.1: Answering security questions

- Enter 2 to 4-digit pins of your choice and click "Summit"

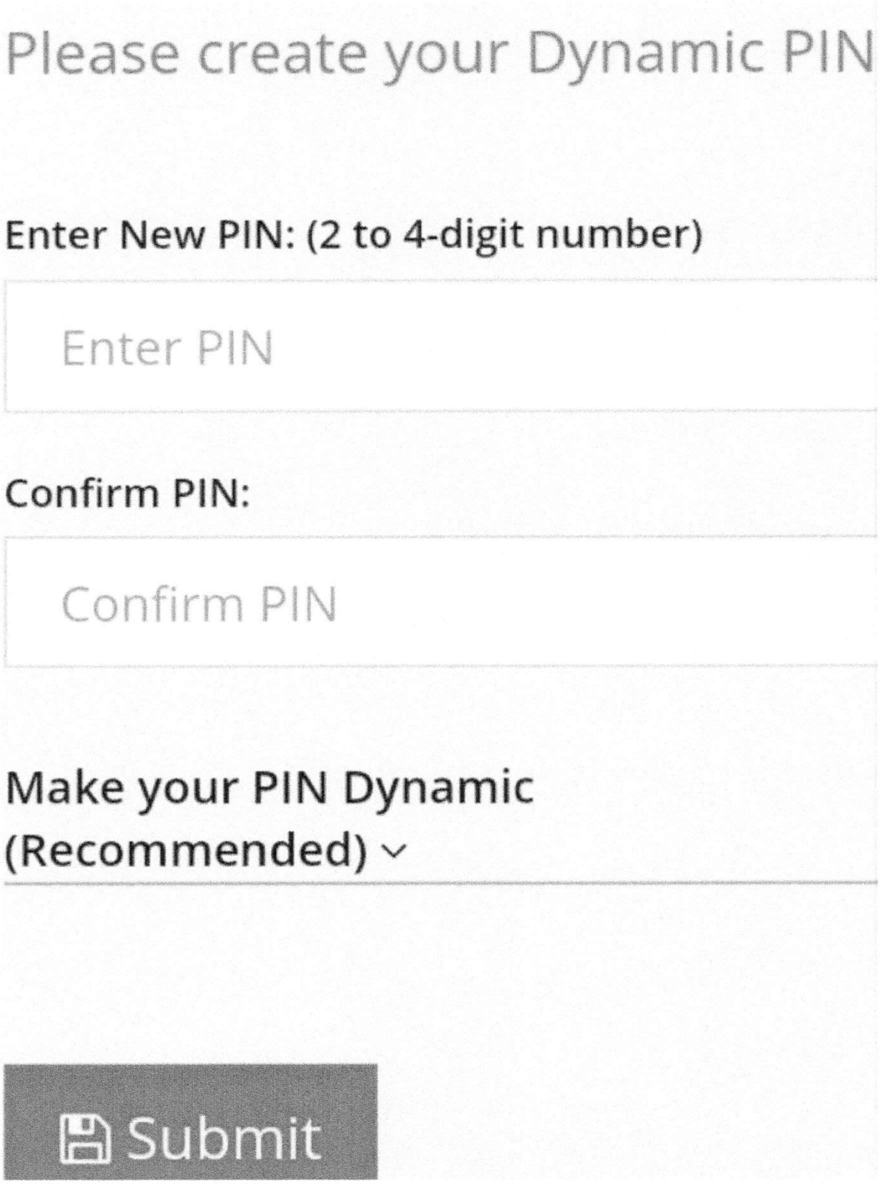

Please create your Dynamic PIN

Enter New PIN: (2 to 4-digit number)

Enter PIN

Confirm PIN:

Confirm PIN

Make your PIN Dynamic (Recommended) ⌄

 Submit

Fig 6.1.2: Creating dynamic pin for security purpose

- Enter the security code sent to your phone number in the space provided for you and hit "Submit".

Security

For your added security, a security c
You need to enter the code in the box bel

Enter Security Code From Your Phone Here

Fig 6.1.3: Screenshot showing space to enter the security code

A congratulatory notification appears on your screen once the system confirms you entered the correct code.

To start receiving and making payments,
Click here to Add An Account

OR

Skip and continue to the Dashboard

Fig 6.1.4: The congratulatory notification that shows on your screen once the system confirms it

The image also shows that you should click on "Add An Account" to add your bank account details.

- Click on "Add An Account" link
- Fill your account details

Add Account

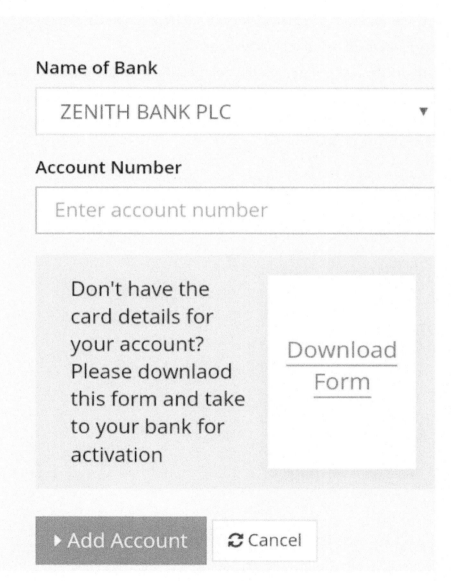

Name of Bank

ZENITH BANK PLC ▼

Account Number

Enter account number

Don't have the card details for your account? Please downlaod this form and take to your bank for activation

Download Form

▶ Add Account   ⟳ Cancel

Fig 6.1.5: Select your bank from the dropdown and add your account number

The account details to fill is your bank account details in Nigeria. It can be Savings or Current account

- Click on Add Account (designed in green color as shown in Fig 6.1.5) after filling your bank account details

- Insert the last 4 digits on the debit card connected to that account and OTP sent to you by the bank for verification, and click submit

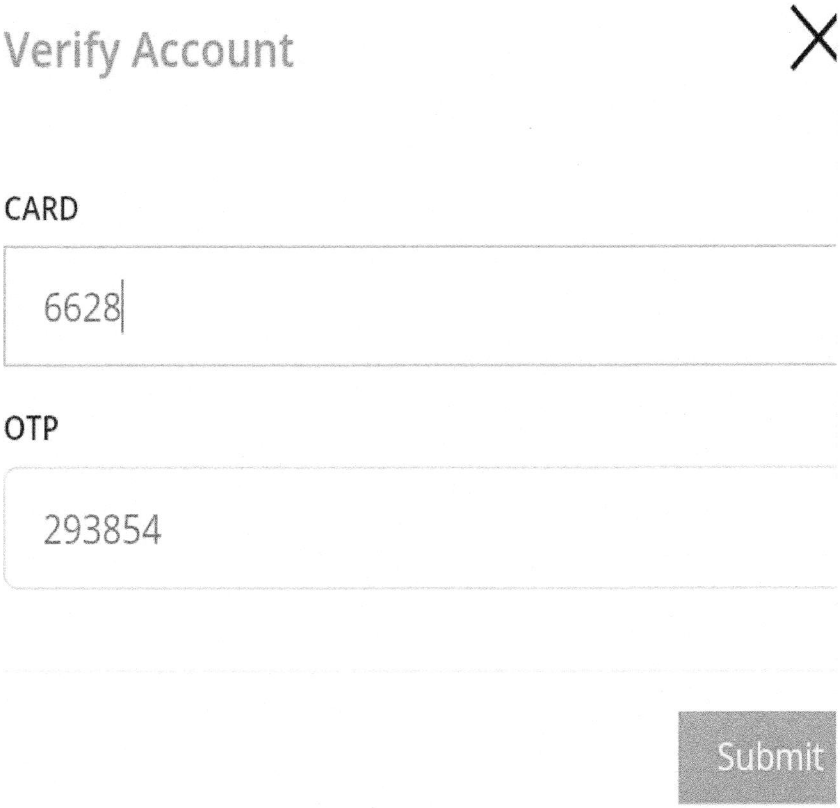

Verify Account

CARD

6628|

OTP

293854

Submit

Fig 6.1.6: Insert the digits and OTP in the right place

- Select "Set up Collection" that appears on the next page

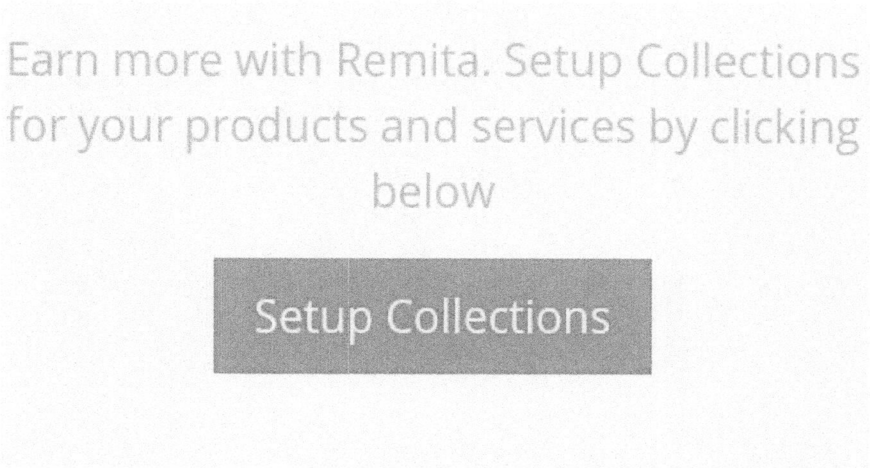

Earn more with Remita. Setup Collections
for your products and services by clicking
below

Setup Collections

Fig 6.1.6: Select "Setup Collection" as shown

- Select "Yes" for the question "Will you be implementing an integration with Remita for your collection" and click "Proceed"

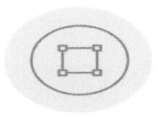

Will you be implementing an integration with Remita for your collections?

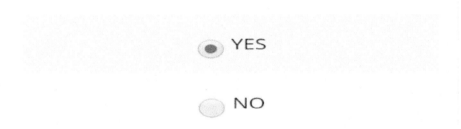

YES

NO

PROCEED

Fig 6.1.7: The question that will show up after clicking "Setup Collection"

- Copy your Public Key and Secret Key, paste and save them in a word processor like Microsoft word or Note.

You will insert the Public Key and Secret Key in Remita-WooCommerce plugin through WordPress dashboard. Do not worry because I will tell you when we get there.

We are Almost Done!

Linking the Public and Secret Keys with Remita-WooCommerce Plugin

To complete this task, do the following:

- Login to your WordPress dashboard

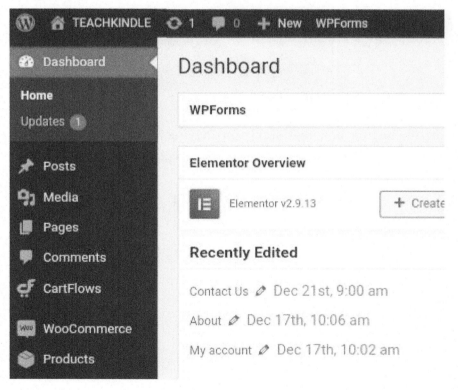

Fig 6.1.8: My WordPress dashboard

- Select Plugins followed by Add New

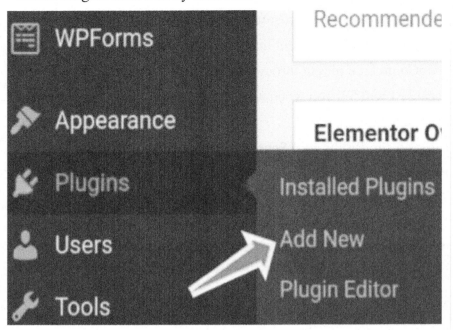

Fig 6.1.9: Selecting Plugins and Add New

- In the search box that shows up having the mode of search as Keywords, type "Remita WooCommerce Payment Plugin"

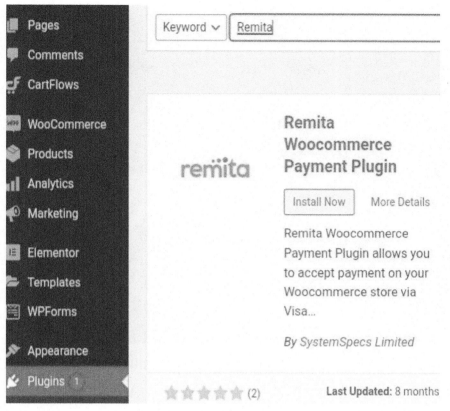

Fig 6.2.1: Searching for "Remita WooCommerce Payment Gateway"

- Click on Install now on the Plugin

- Click on Activate

- Select WooCommerce screen option

Fig 6.2.2: Selecting "WooCommerce" screen option

- Select Settings

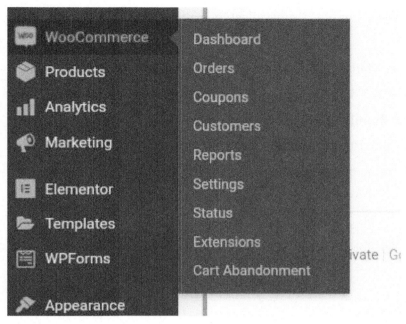

Fig 6.2.3: Selecting WooCommerce Settings (Select Settings which is after "Reports")

When you click on settings, you will be taken to the Payment Settings.

- Click on the button in same line with Remita to Enable it.

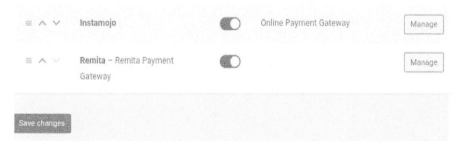

Fig 6.2.4: Enabling Remita Payment Gateway by clicking on the button to turn purple color

Disable other payment gateways that might have been enabled before. For example, I must disable Instamojo as seen in the image above.

- Click on Manage or setup by the right-hand side of the Remita

From Fig 6.2.4, I have to click on "Manage" which is in the same line with Remita to insert required information.

- Insert the Public and the Secret keys we generated from Rita website in the boxes appropriately.

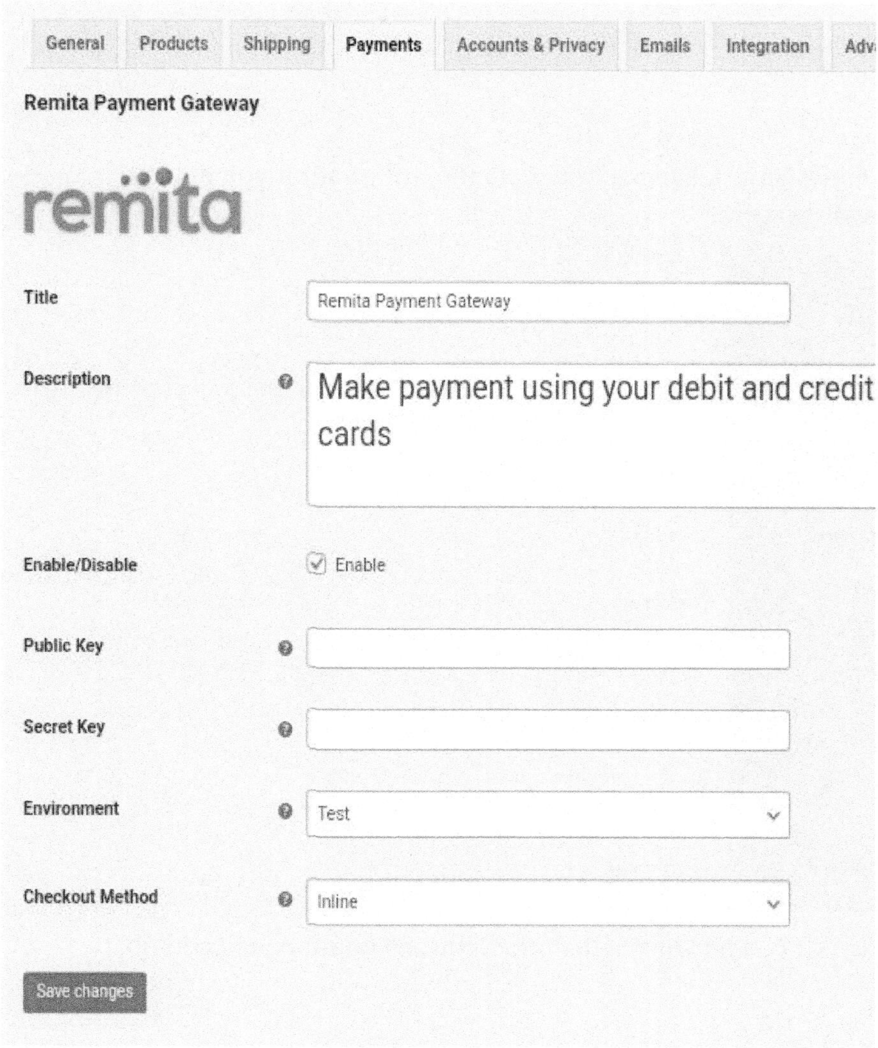

| General | Products | Shipping | **Payments** | Accounts & Privacy | Emails | Integration | Adv |

Remita Payment Gateway

remita

Title	Remita Payment Gateway
Description	❷ Make payment using your debit and credit cards
Enable/Disable	✓ Enable
Public Key	❷
Secret Key	❷
Environment	❷ Test ⌄
Checkout Method	❷ Inline ⌄

Save changes

Fig 6.2.5: Paste the Public and Secret Keys you were given when you created account on Remita website into the boxes.

- Click Save Changes to update the information you entered

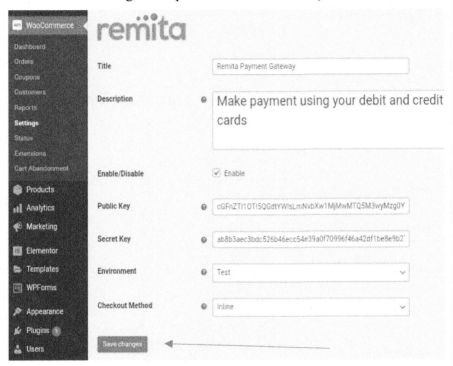

Fig 6.2.6: The "Save Changes" button should be clicked on

- Click on General Settings heading

-Set all the information needed in the General Settings to be directed to Nigeria.

Fig 6.2.7: General Settings and information partially completed shown.

Your contact address, location, targeted customers and other information should be directed to Nigeria. Also, your currency should be in Nigerian currency, Naira.

- Save the changes you made by clicking on "Save Changes"

You can then visit the ecommerce website you are building and try to buy a product. It will work perfectly.

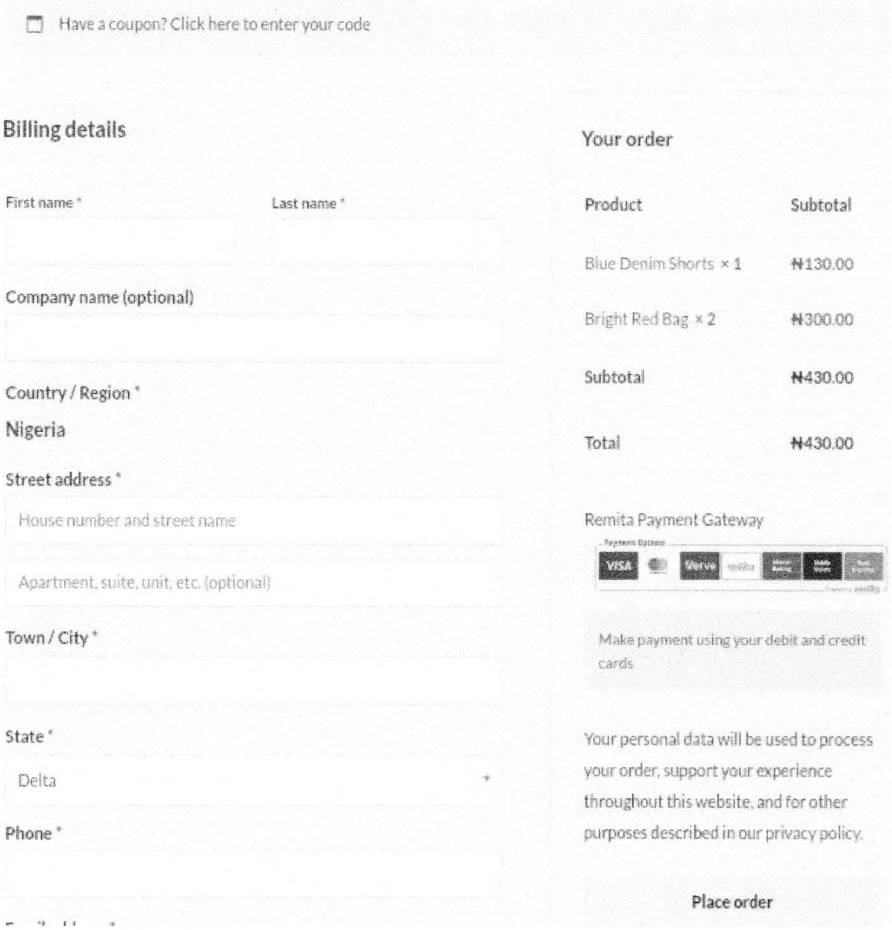

☐ Have a coupon? Click here to enter your code

Billing details

First name *

Last name *

Company name (optional)

Country / Region *

Nigeria

Street address *

House number and street name

Apartment, suite, unit, etc. (optional)

Town / City *

State *

Delta

Phone *

Your order

Product	Subtotal
Blue Denim Shorts × 1	₦130.00
Bright Red Bag × 2	₦300.00
Subtotal	₦430.00
Total	₦430.00

Remita Payment Gateway

VISA ⬤ Verve resitha

Make payment using your debit and credit cards

Your personal data will be used to process your order, support your experience throughout this website, and for other purposes described in our privacy policy.

Place order

Fig 6.2.8: Attempt to place order on my ecommerce website after choosing Remita as payment gateway

In that image, I hope you see Remita payment gateway as a payment method. That shows that everything is working fine.

What of if you want to Enable Direct Bank Transfer on the Nigerian Ecommerce Website?

It is possible. Just click on WooCommerce, Select Settings and then enable Direct Bank Transfer. Fill your bank account information. Save and the deal is done.

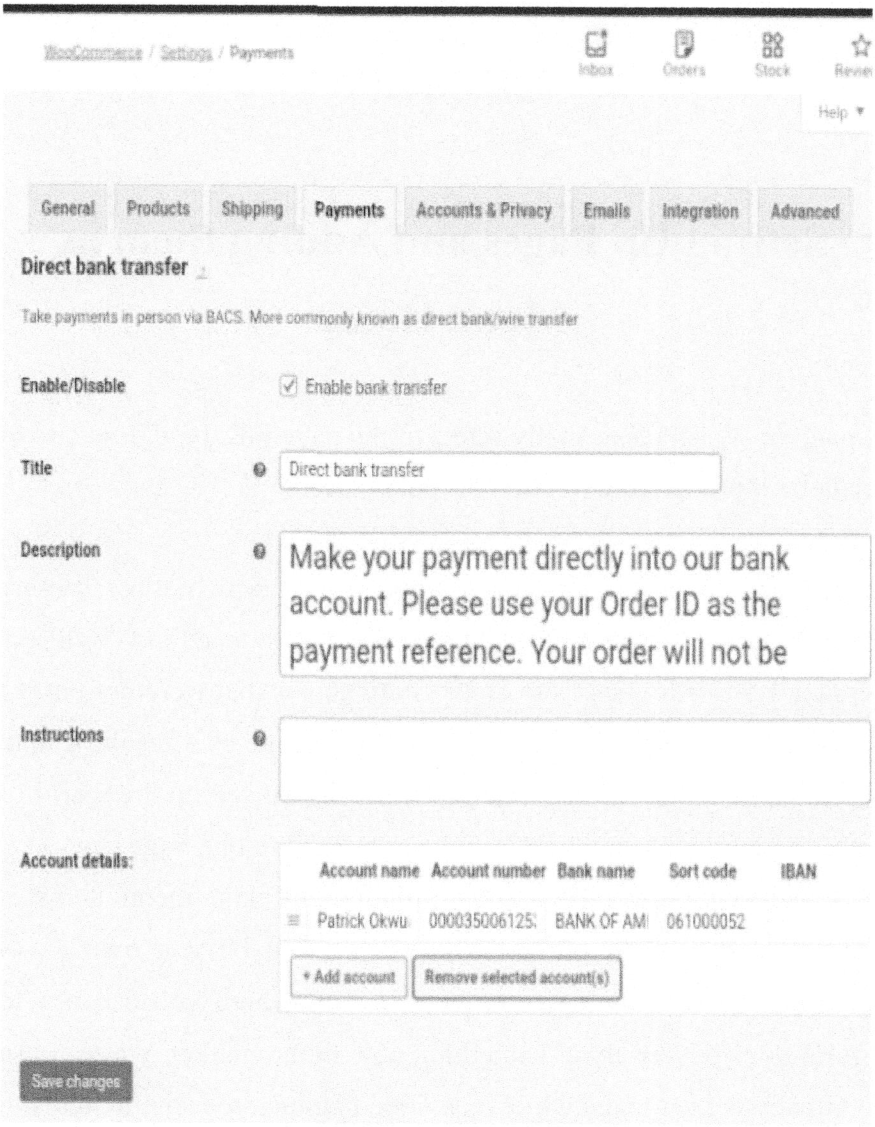

Inbox   Orders   Stock   Revie

Help ▼

| General | Products | Shipping | **Payments** | Accounts & Privacy | Emails | Integration | Advanced |

Direct bank transfer

Take payments in person via BACS. More commonly known as direct bank/wire transfer

Enable/Disable   ☑ Enable bank transfer

Title   ❓   Direct bank transfer

Description   ❓

Make your payment directly into our bank account. Please use your Order ID as the payment reference. Your order will not be

Instructions   ❓

Account details:

Account name	Account number	Bank name	Sort code	IBAN
≡ Patrick Okwu	000035006125:	BANK OF AM!	061000052	

[+ Add account] [Remove selected account(s)]

[Save changes]

Fig 6.2.9: Complete the account details section and save, and Direct Bank Transfer will be activated on your ecommerce website

Chapter 7

Setting Up Pages and Adding them as Menu Items

A page in WordPress usually refers to the page post type. It is one of the default pre-defined WordPress post types.

WordPress started out as simple blogging tool which allowed users to write posts. In the year 2005, Pages were introduced in WordPress version 1.5 to allow users to create static pages that were not part of their blog posts. In life, there is room for change as a result of that, WordPress brought in that change which has spiced up the world of website building. Many posts can be contained in one Page.

Why we need few pages to be among our main menu items is because it can be helpful in some cases. Maybe you own an e-commerce website and you want a section where you can use to inform your buyers about something new in the market, you can use an already created page which you added among your menu items to do so. You can name that menu item to be "Something New".

Example of main menu of a website containing menu items is the image below.

Fig 7: Image shows the menu items of our learning website teachkindle.com

In the image, Home, Store, Men, Women, Accessories, Account, About and Contact Us are all menu items. Before they were added as menu items, some were first created as pages while some others as categories. I hope am not stressing you much. Not to worry because I will get to where I will teach more on categories in the later chapter.

I this chapter, I will take you step by step on how to create Pages in WordPress. Also, I will explain in detail on how you can add these created pages to your website main menu. Note that Astra themes come with already created pages, but I will create a fresh page for the purpose of this teaching.

Practical: Step by Step Guide in Creating a Page

Following the following steps to create a page:

- Login to your WordPress admin area/dashboard

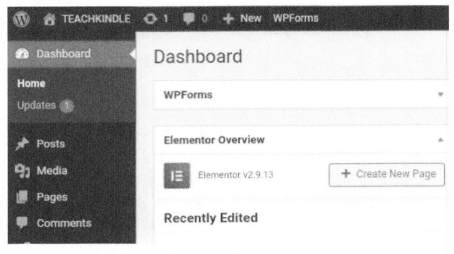

Fig 7.1: The dashboard of my WordPress

You can login by using then administrative URL you were given when you finished installing and setting up your WordPress account through control panel. The format of administrative URL is www.mywebsite.com/wp-admin. Example, the administrative URL an using to teach you here is: ww.teachkindle.com/wp-admin/

- Select Pages screen option

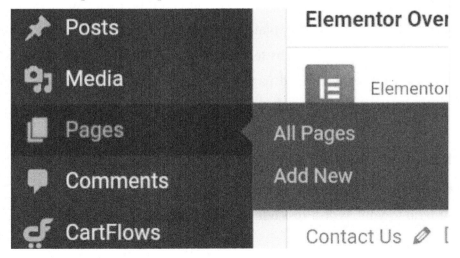

Fig 7.2: As you click on Pages, the two sub-screen options appear

- Select Add New

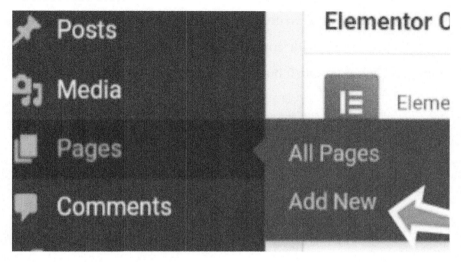

Fig 7.3: "Add New" shown.

- Add the Title of the Page, example "Something New"

As the new page opens, add the title of the page in the space provided for you by the system.

Fig 7.4: Space to add page title shown

- Compose your contents

Click on the space written "start writing or type/to choose a block" as shown in Fig 7.4 and start writing what you want to have in your page body.

- Click on Publish after writing

When you are done with composing or writing the content of your page, just click on publish button by the right-hand side.

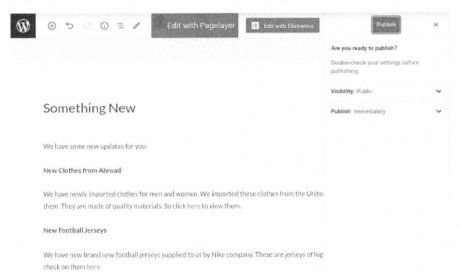

Fig 7.5: Image shows the "Publish" button by the right, title and page body (content)

With the above steps, you can create a page or even pages. You can see below on how the page I create which I titled "Something New" looks like on my e-commerce website.

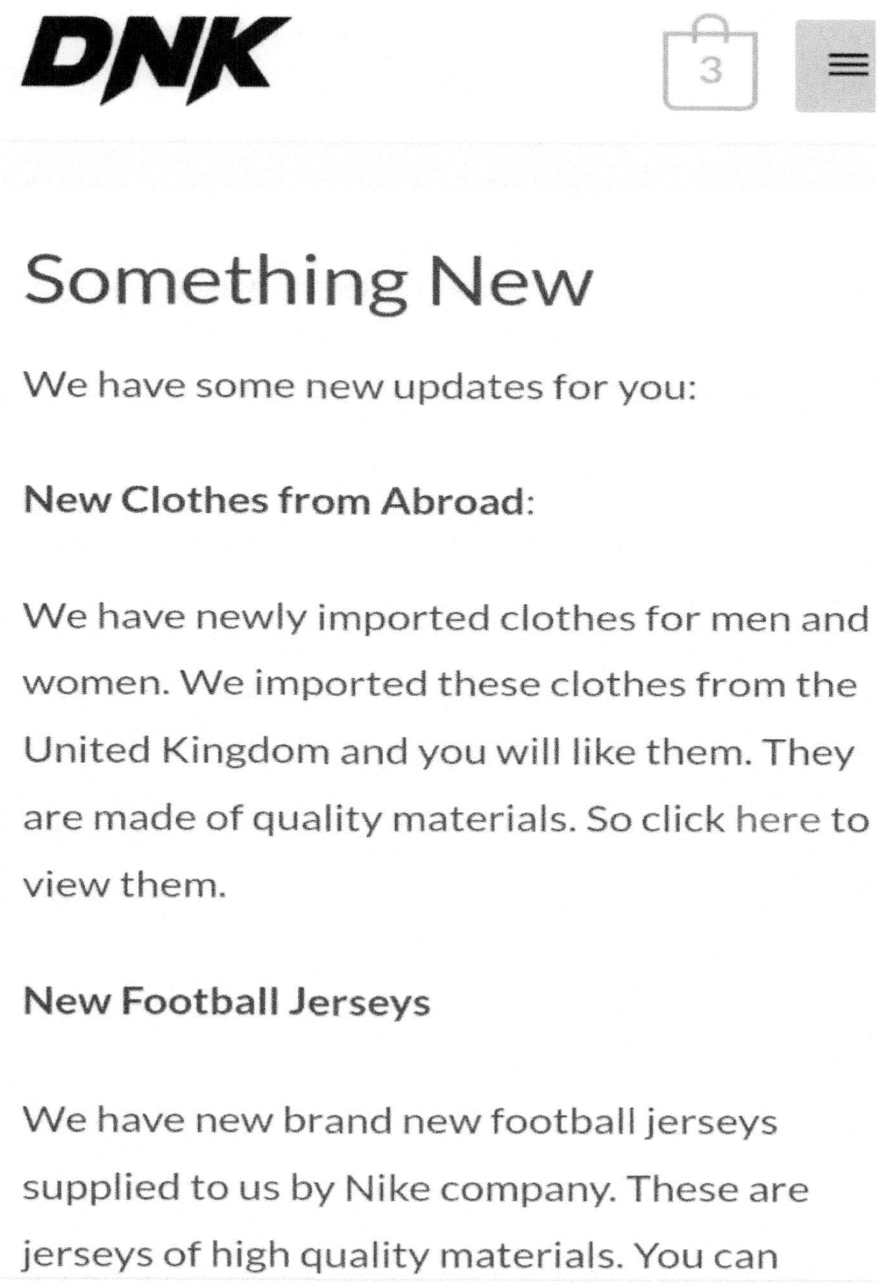

Something New

We have some new updates for you:

New Clothes from Abroad:

We have newly imported clothes for men and women. We imported these clothes from the United Kingdom and you will like them. They are made of quality materials. So click here to view them.

New Football Jerseys

We have new brand new football jerseys supplied to us by Nike company. These are jerseys of high quality materials. You can

Fig 7.6: Screenshot of my newly created page titled "Something New" as it appears on my website

Note: You can update created pages on your website any time you feel like doing so. To do this, log in to your WordPress dashboard, select Pages, then All pages. Look for the Page you want to update as the are arranged by their names. The next is that you hover round the page and you will see "Edit" button, click on it and the page will open. You can make the necessary change you want to make at that point and then click on "Update" button for your updated information to be saved. This is simple explanation and I believe you understand it.

How to Add Created Page to the Main Menu of your E-Commerce Website

It is important to learn this area. Many beginners in website building sometimes run into problem when they do not have any manual guiding them to complete the task in this section but I will handle the challenge here. To add the created page to your website menu, do the following:

- Sign into your WordPress dashboard or just click on Dashboard if you are already signed in to WordPress

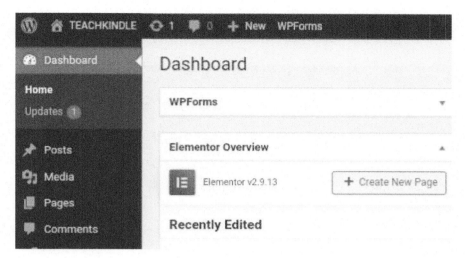

Fig 7.7: My WordPress admin dashboard

- Open a new tab in your browser

Please make sure you have already signed in to your WordPress as directed in stage one before opening a new tab in the same browser you are using. This will help us achieve our task at the end

- Type in the URL of your website in the newly opened tab and search

Example, I have to type the URL of my own website which I am using for this teaching, that is www.teachkindle.com

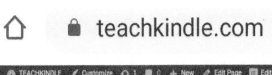

Fig 7.8: The homepage of my website after I typed in my website URL and hit enter key of my keyboard

- Look on the top part of the website and select "Customize"

Fig 7.9: Select "Customize" as shown by the arrow

- Select Menus from the page that opens

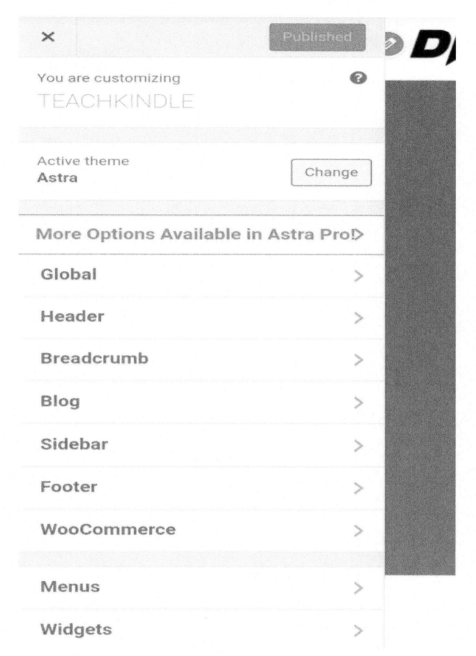

Fig 7.1.1: Select Menus as shown on the image (Menus appears before Widgets on the image)

- Select Main Menu

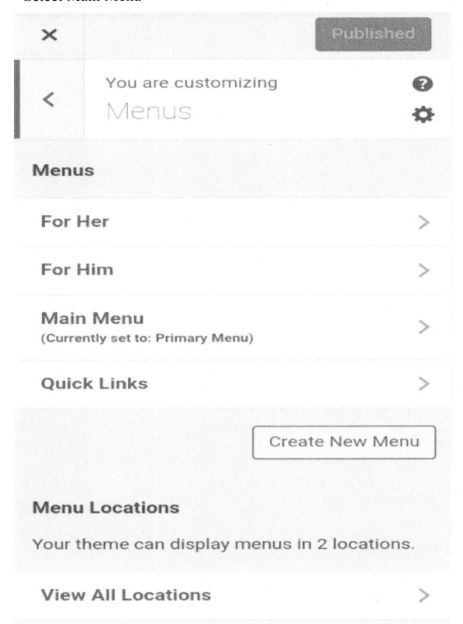

Fig 7.1.2: Select Main Menu from the other options

- Select "Add Item"

You are to select "Add Item" that appears at the bottom for you to be allowed to add any menu item in the primary menu.

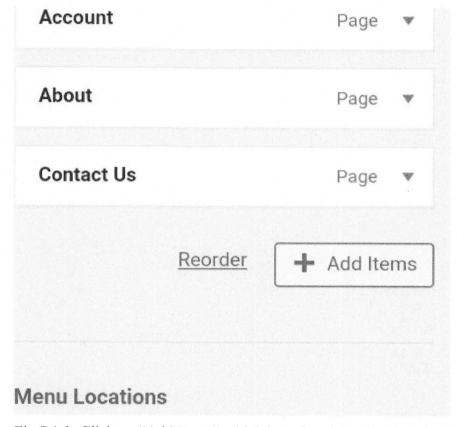

Fig 7.1.3: Click on "Add Items" which has plus sign in its front

- From the new window that opens, search for the page you want to add, which is "Something New" in this teaching

- Select the page by clicking on it ("Something New")

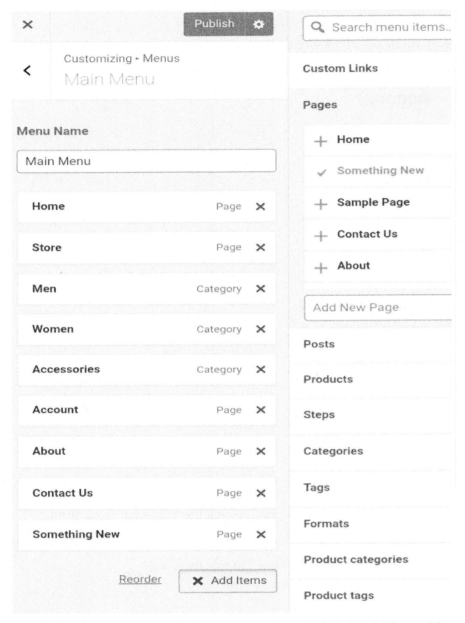

Fig 7.1.4: Selecting the page I want to add which I titled "Something New"

From Fig 7.1.4, when I clicked on "Something New" by the right-hand side group which I was adding, it was marked "good" and then added to the left-hand side as shown on the image as well. So, it joined the set of the active menu items in Main Menu.

- Click on Publish button

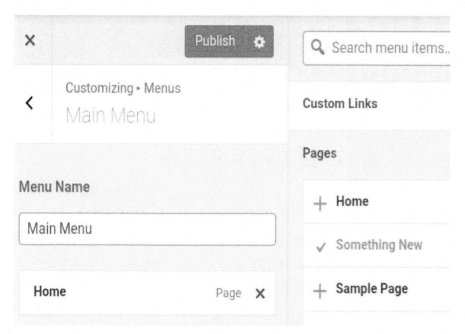

Fig 7.1.5: Click on the Publish button on top to save the added item

You can also arrange the menu items the way you want to order them before clicking on Publish.

You can visit your website homepage to see the newly added page in the menu. Using my example, if I visit my website, www.teachkindle.com, I will see "Something New" among the main menu items.

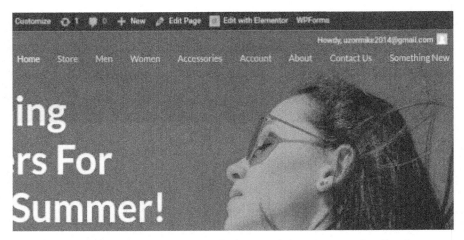

Fig 7.1.6: My e-commerce website main menu as it displays my newly added page item "Something New" (the last menu item by the right) along the other previously existing items.

You can decide to create as many pages as possible which you want to add to your e-commerce website as menu items. Just follow my guide here and you will get the job done. Also know that you can create categories which can also be added in a menu. We will discuss more on that in a later chapter.

Chapter 8

Product Section of WooCommerce and the use in Building E-commerce Website

Products are the main thing customers search for whenever they visit any e-commerce website. No products, no e-commerce website. As a result of this, you must pay attention to this part of our discussion. I will take you on a journey as we dig deeper into this chapter. There are a lot you need to learn from this chapter.

Products can be grouped into categories through WooCommerce plugin. Product categories and tags work the same way as normal categories and tags you have when writing posts in WordPress. They can be created, edited, and selected at any time. This can be done when you first create a product or come back and edit it or the category/tag specifically.

To see all the products you have in your WordPress, Sign into your WordPress dashboard, under WooCommerce screen option, select Products and then All Products. This action will display the products you have.

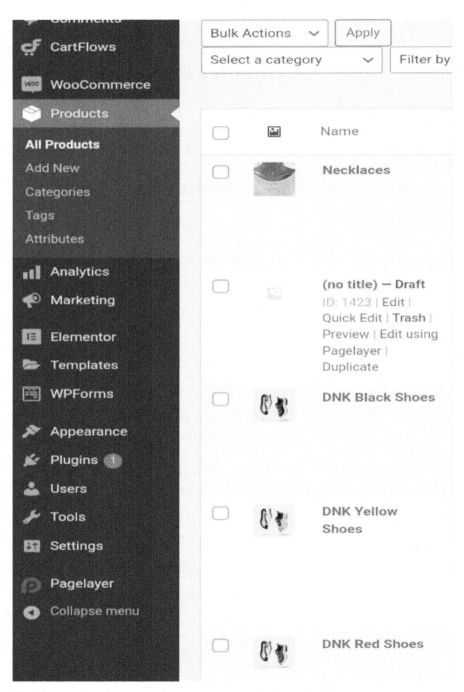

Fig 8: Some of the Products in my "Product" section

You can select next page and more to see all your products. In fact, if you have many products on your website, you can get tired selecting Next button upon Next button just to see all of them.

Types of Products sold on E-commerce Websites

With attributes and categories setup and stock management configured, we can begin adding products. When adding a product, the first thing to decide is what type of product it is.

Simple – covers the vast majority of any products you may sell. Simple products are shipped and have no options. For example, a book.

Grouped – a collection of related products that can be purchased individually and only consist of simple products. For example, a set of six drinking glasses, and a set of long sleeve shirts.

Virtual – one that doesn't require shipping. For example, a service. Enabling this disables all shipping related fields such as shipping dimensions of the product. A virtual product will also not trigger the shipping calculator in cart and checkout.

Downloadable – activates additional fields where you can provide a downloadable file. After a successful purchase, customers are given a downloadable file as a link in the order notification email. This is suitable, for example, for a digital album, PDF magazine, or photo.

External or Affiliate – one that you list and describe on your website but is sold elsewhere.

Variable – a product with variations, each of which may have a different SKU, price, stock option, etc. For example, a t-shirt available in different colors and/or sizes.

Terms in Products Section

Products section of WooCommerce plugin has some components in it. In this subheading, I will be explaining these terms. That will help your understanding on Products and guide you on what to do, were to click and how to select the best option for a particular task.

You cannot imagine the stress I passed through one night trying to use a tool under Products one day when I was trying to master this section. I was stressed out that night trying to complete one task that day. I got it right at the end, but it was not easy for me that day. Please, I do not want you to pass through that same stress and that is one of the essences of writing this book for you to know how to do some things on e-commerce website building in a less stressful way.

Fig 8.1: Screenshot showing the components of Products section

As shown in the screenshot above, Products section is made up of major components. These components are All Products, Add New, Categories, Tags and Attributes. Each of these components also have their own components. I will do well to explain them and their use.

All Products

As explained earlier in this chapter, All Products tab shows all the products that are existing in your store. It also contains the drafted products which you are yet to publish on your online store. In Fig 8.1, I showed you part of the products in All Products tab. If I elaborated the image without cutting some part of it, you would have seen the products name, the categories they are added to, the price of each product, tag on each product, date added, and whether in stock or not.

Add New

This feature allows you to add as many products you want as possible. When you select Add New, a new page opens which allows you to complete a specific task. With this feature, you can give a product a title, add the product into any category of your choice, add product description, choose a product type, add the image of the product which is called product image, add tag to the product if you want to, add product price and then publish the product.

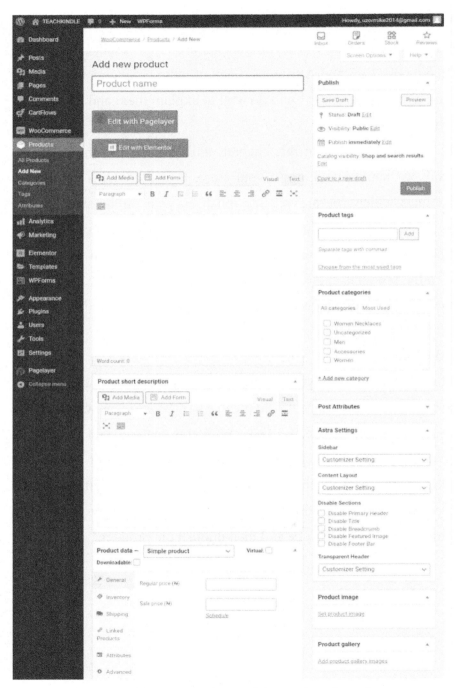

Fig 8.2: The page that opens when Add New is selected

I want you to take a good look at that Product data section of that Fig 8.2 above. You see that part that allows you to add price of your product, sometimes most beginners find it difficult to locate when they want to add price to their product. The price section is usually closed by default.

It appears as shown in the screenshot below:

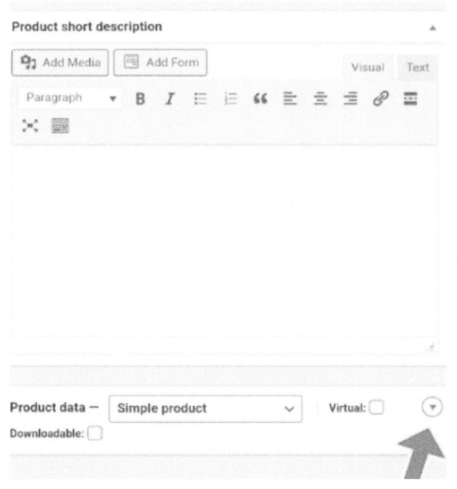

Fig 8.3: The default appearance of Product data section

It is when click at the dropdown at the right-hand side that the section that will allow you to add the price of the product will display. That is as seen in the image below:

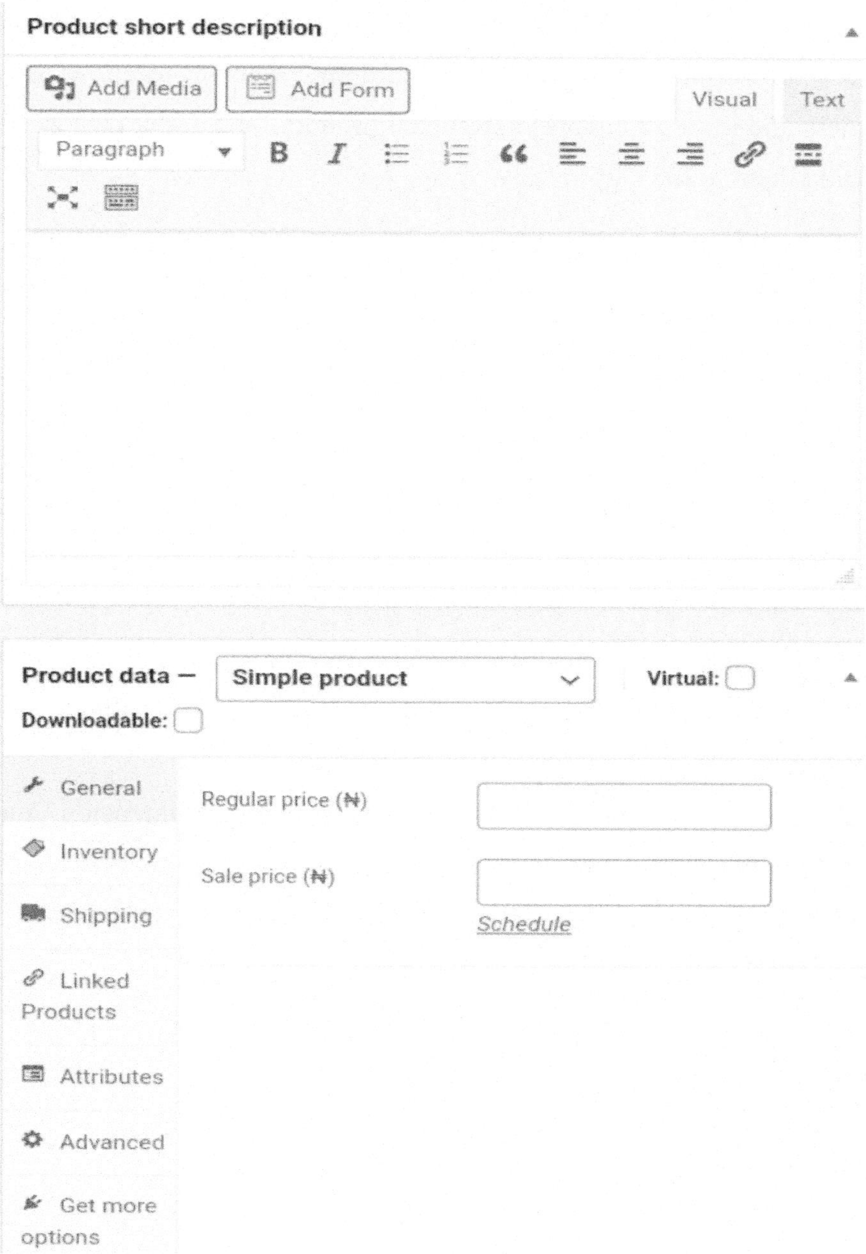

Product short description

🗣 Add Media	🖼 Add Form		Visual	Text

Paragraph ▾   **B**   *I*   ☰   ☰   66   ☰   ☰   ☰   🔗   ☰
⤢   ⌨

Product data —   Simple product   ⌄   Virtual: ⬜   ▲

Downloadable: ⬜

🔧 General	Regular price (₦)	[ ]
🔷 Inventory		
🚚 Shipping	Sale price (₦)	[ ]
🔗 Linked Products		*Schedule*
🖼 Attributes		
⚙ Advanced		
⚑ Get more options		

Fig 8.4: Product data section that allows you to add price to your products.

The inventory section of Product data panel allows you to manage stock for the product individually and define whether to allow back orders and more. It enables you to sell products and allow customers to add them to the cart to buy.

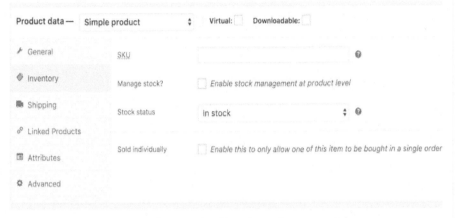

Fig 8.5: Inventory section under Product data panel

Options when stock management at product level is disabled, you are responsible for updating the Stock Status.

Shipping section allows you to choose the weight, dimension, and the shipping class of the product you are adding. Shipping classes are used by certain shipping methods to group similar products.

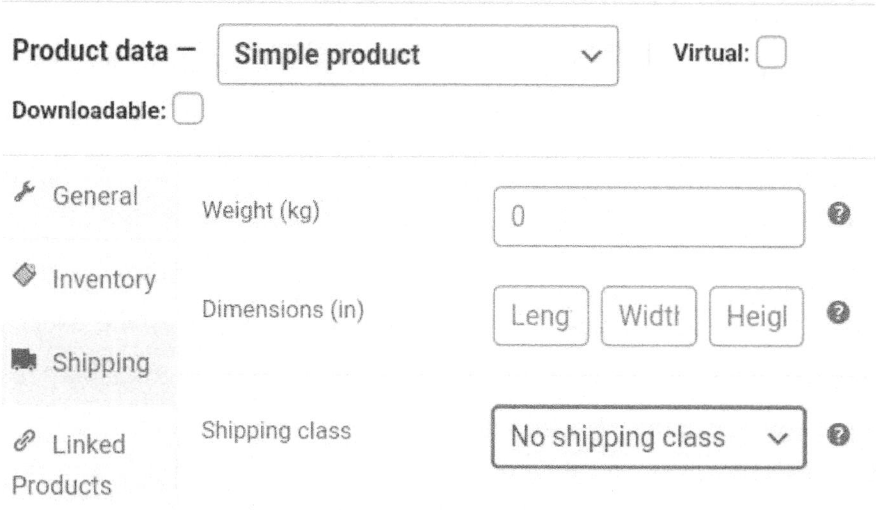

Product data — | Simple product ⌄ | Virtual: ☐

Downloadable: ☐

🔧 General

Weight (kg) | 0 | ❷

💎 Inventory

Dimensions (in) | Leng | Widtl | Heigl | ❷

🚚 Shipping

🔗 Linked Products

Shipping class | No shipping class ⌄ | ❷

Fig 8.6: The components of the Shipping section under Product data

For linked product section, using up-sells and cross-sells, you can cross promote your products. They can be added by searching for a particular product and selecting the product from the dropdown list.

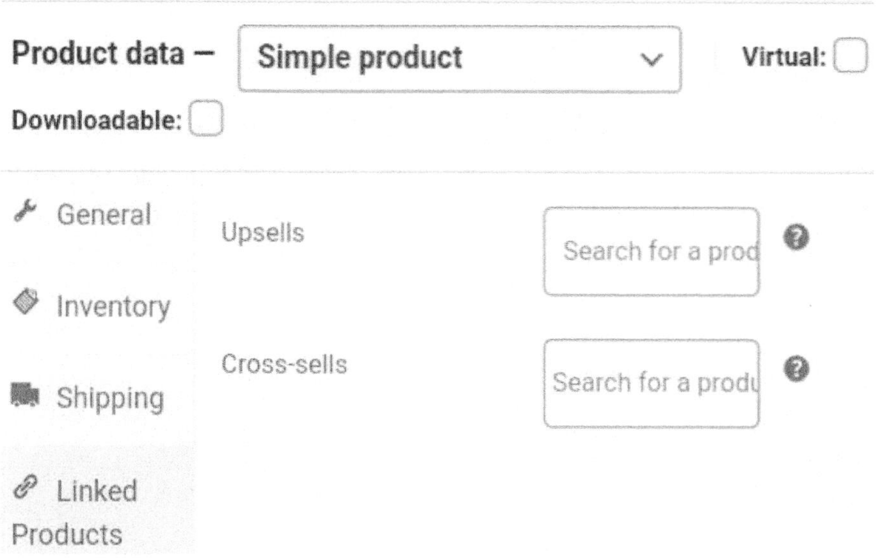

Product data — | Simple product ⌄ | Virtual: ☐

Downloadable: ☐

🔧 General

Upsells | Search for a prod ❷

💎 Inventory

Cross-sells | Search for a produ ❷

🚚 Shipping

🔗 Linked Products

Fig 8.7: The screenshot of Linked Products under Product data

Have you viewed a product on e-commerce website, and you see something like "Buy related product"? If you have, that function is created through "Linked Products" of Product data if that site was built using WordPress/WooCommerce tools.

Up-sells are displayed on the product details page. These are products that you may wish to encourage users to upgrade, based on the product they are currently viewing. For example, if the user is viewing the coffee product listing page, you may want to display tea kettles on that same page as an up-sell.

Attributes is another part of Product data. On the Attributes tab, you can assign details to a product. You will see a select box containing global attribute sets you created (e.g., platform).

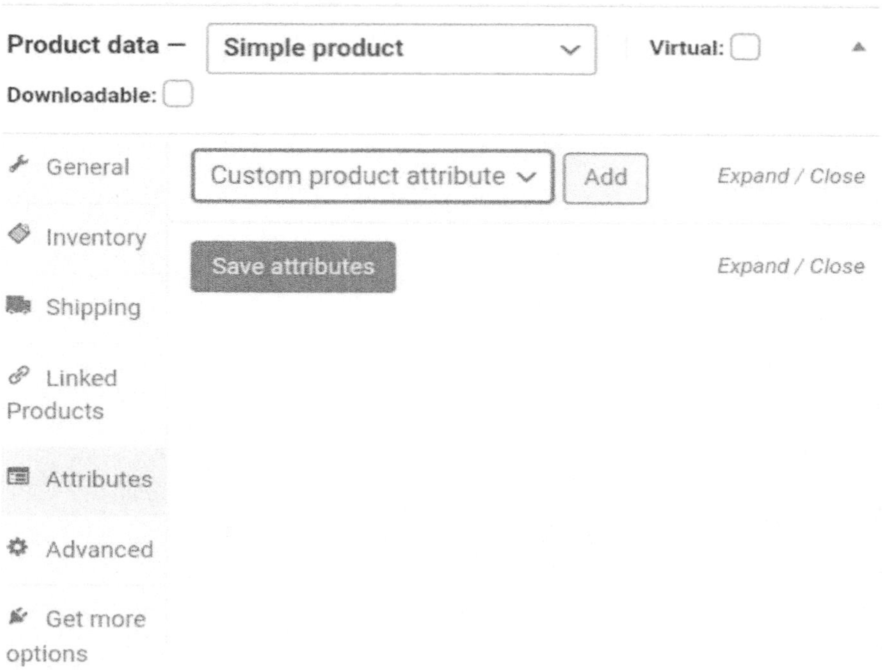

Product data — | Simple product ∨ | Virtual: ⬚ ▲

Downloadable: ⬚

🔧 General | Custom product attribute ∨ | Add | *Expand / Close*

◈ Inventory | Save attributes | *Expand / Close*

🚚 Shipping

🔗 Linked Products

▦ Attributes

⚙ Advanced

📣 Get more options

Fig 8.8: Screenshot showing what is contained in Attributes section

Once you have chosen an attribute from the select box, click add and apply the terms attached to that attribute (e.g., Nintendo DS) to the product. You can hide the attribute on the frontend by leaving the Visible checkbox unticked.

Custom attributes can also be applied by choosing Custom product attribute from the select box. These are added at the product level and won't be available in layered navigation or other products.

Let me make it more practical, if I want to write an attribute on a particular product I want to setup, I will click on that dropdown shown in Fig 8.8 and then select "Custom Product attribute as you can see in the same image. I then click on "Add" button as shown as well. Once done, the screenshot below appears:

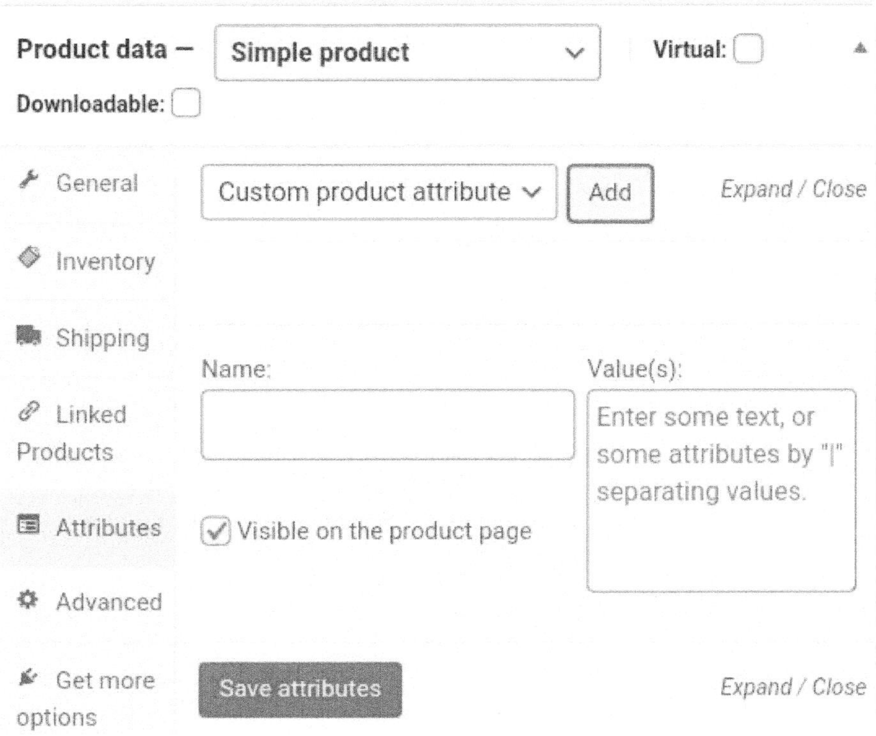

Fig 8.9: Writing an attribute on a product

You can give that product attribute name like "Standard", tick the option "Visible on the product Page" and then write a statement in the box under "Value(s)" like "The product is a replica of quality". With this exercise, you have added complete attribute to the product.

Practical: Step by Step guide in Adding Products to your E-Commerce Website

To add Products which you want to sell to customers on your e-commerce store, follow these steps:

- Login to your WordPress admin dashboard or click on dashboard if you already working in it

- Under WooCommerce, select Products and followed by Add New

Fig 8.1.1: When Product is selected

- Insert the title of the product you want to publish

Example of title of the product can be "Tiny Gold Initial Heart Necklace", and I will be teaching with this title in this section. Note that the title of your product can be shorter than the one I used as an example.

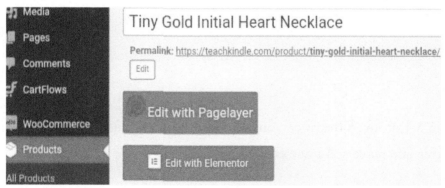

Fig 8.1.2: Inserted the product title as "Tiny Gold Initial Heart Necklace"

- Type description of the product in the space provided for that.

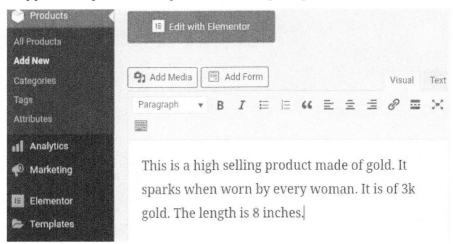

Fig 8.1.3: Typing of the description of my product in progress.

- Set the price of the product in the Product data section

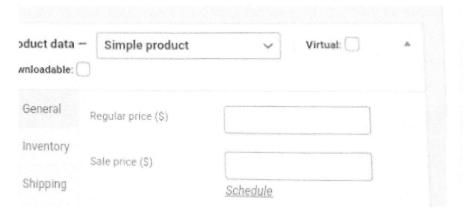

Fig 8.1.4: Insert the price you want to sell your product in the regular price and leave sell price empty

- Add a category you want the product to appear under if you wish and have already created any.

If you are making use of Astra theme in your WordPress to build your e-commerce website, product categories are positioned at the right-hand side as you are adding a new product.

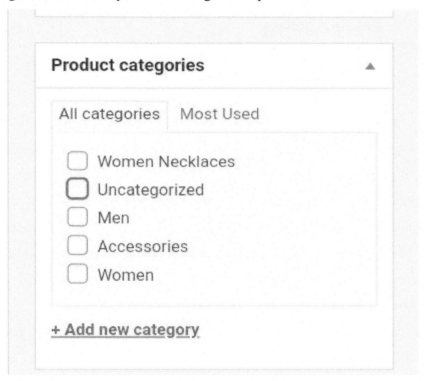

Fig 8.1.5: You can choose a category from the list of existing categories if the theme you are using on your website created some that fits into your product already.

- Set up product image

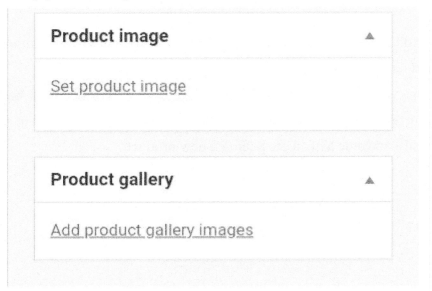

Fig 8.1.6: The tab to choose a product Image is located at the bottom part of your right-hand side

Product image is the image of the product you want to add to your online store. Please make sure the picture is clear and attracting. It is one of the properties that make customers buy products from online stores. You can hire a graphic professional to give your images touches before upload.

You can upload the image from your computer or from your WordPress image gallery if it is there.

- Click on Publish button

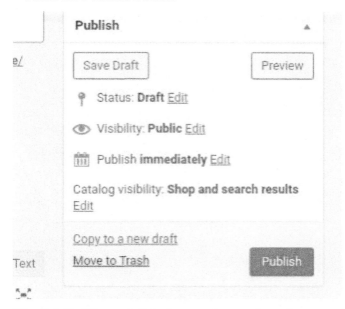

Fig 8.1.7: The publish button located at the top right corner of the product publishing page

After checking and you find out that everything is in place, hit publish button to publish your product. If you visit the store page of your e-commerce website, you will see your newly published product there.

So, if I check in the store section of my website, I will see my newly published product which I named "Tiny Gold Initial Heart Necklace"

Fig 8.1.8: The way the added product displays in the store of my teaching website, www.teachkindle.com

As you want to build a working e-commerce website, use this teaching I gave you in this section to add as many products as you want on your e-commerce or your clients e-commerce websites. I hope the steps are simple and easy to practice with? I believe you will build quality e-commerce stores with this teaching. Do not forget to write to me if any form of issue comes up.

How to Create Product Categories

Let us assume that you are building an e-commerce website that is made up of 3 major categories. The three major categories are DIY Books, Fashion, and Electronics. So, I want you to build 3 categories of the 3 major keywords. Or if I decide to build with the keywords on my own, how will I do it?

To create each of the categories, follow the steps below:

- Login to youth WordPress admin dashboard
- Select Products under WooCommerce screen option
- Select categories

Fig 8.1.9: Select Categories which is the number 3 in the list

- Add a Category name

Type in a category name in the title space

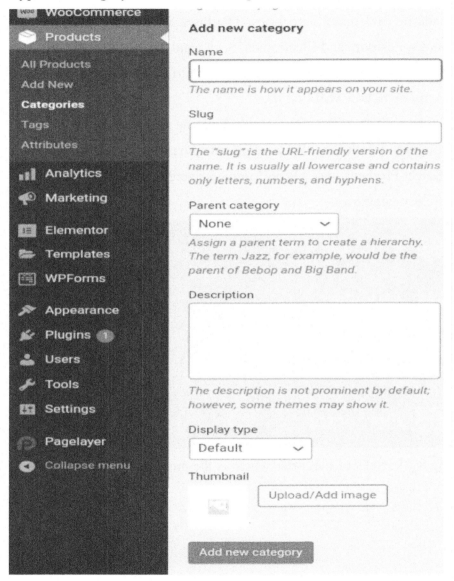

Fig 8.2.1: Type in the name you want the category to bear in the space "Name"

I can decide to type DIY Books in the title space and create it first. This means that after creation I can include some of my products in that category which must be "do it yourself books" (DIY Books).

- Add slug if you wish otherwise the system will generate one

The "slug" is the URL-friendly version of the name. It is usually all lowercase and contains only letters, numbers, and hyphens. I can decide to add diybooks in my slug in respect to the DIY Books category I want to create. When I do so, the URL to that category becomes www.teachkindle.com/diybooks

Fig 8.2.2: Add Slug name in that space

- In the section of Parent Category, just select none unless you have one to add.

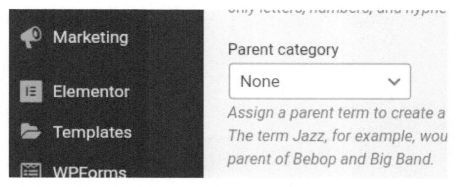

Fig 8.2.3: Selection of parent category option

If you want to add this category under existing category, you can choose one from the drop down, otherwise, you select none.

- Write a short description of the category

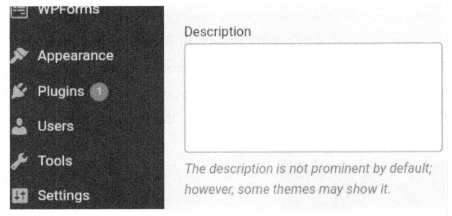

Fig 8.2.4: The description section of the Category

Since am building DIY Books category in this teaching, I can give this category small description like "In this section of our store, we have sound do it yourself books. You can pick any of your interest and read. You can also contact the authors if you run into issues"

- In the thumbnail section, upload any image from your computer or image library.

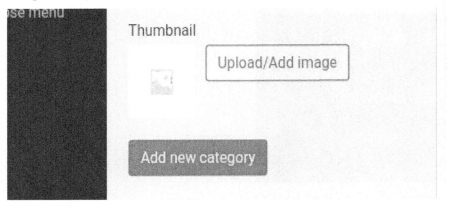

Fig 8.2.5: Thumbnail section shown

The image should reflect what the category is about.

- Click on Add new category which is at the bottom.

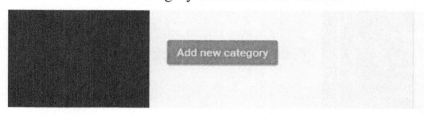

Fig 8.2.6: The "Add new category" button.

The position of the Add new Category is at the button part of the category page. It comes after "Thumbnail" as shown in Fig 8.2.5.

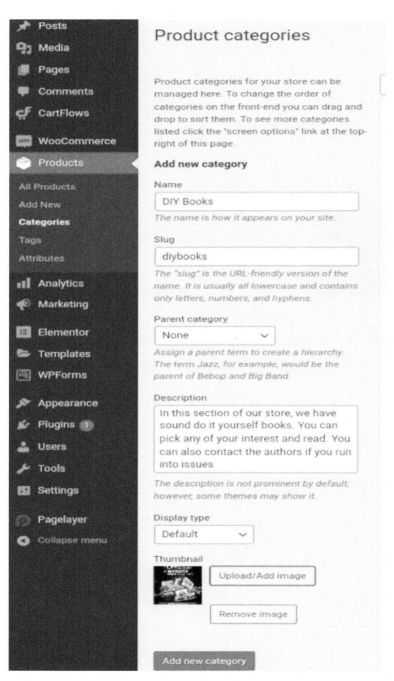

Fig 8.2.7: Completely filled "DIY Books" category

Once I hit the "Add new category" button, the "DIY Books" category is created immediately and then transferred to the category section of WooCommerce.

Another fresh page opens which allows you to start creating other categories if you wish. So, with my illustration here, I can fill in the information for the "Fashion" and after it is created then fill that of "Electronics" category.

Follow this same step to add other categories you want to add. It is a simple task.

Chapter 9

Designing E-Commerce Webpages with Elementor and the Design of other Sections

Quote from elementor website: "Elementor comes with all the designer tools you might need. Design responsive pixel-perfect layouts like you never thought possible on WordPress". Indeed, elementor page builder is a great tool. It has brought in great look to many websites built in the recent time. Elementor is cool to use.

With elementor, you can animate any part of your site with parallax, mouse effects and many other powerful animations and interactions. You can play around with the image settings and add amazing effects to it.

Elementor plugin which I have taught you how to install allows you to choose from 26 different shape dividers to create eye-catching backgrounds. The company has team of talented graphic designers. The company's talented team of designers have worked hard to give you cutting-edge templates for nearly every niche.

There is free and pro version of elementor page builder. In the free version, you do not need to pay any money to use it. But for the pro version of elementor, you are to pay before you are permitted to make use of it.

Elementor pro version has subscription intervals. You can decide to subscribe monthly or annually. The screenshot below shows how much elementor charges per month for the pro version and the number of websites it can be used on.

PERSONAL

For 1 Site

$4.10/month

BUY NOW

Billed Annually

PLUS

For 3 Sites

$8.25/month

BUY NOW

Billed Annually

EXPERT

For 1,000 Sites

$
16.60/month

BUY NOW

Billed Annually

Fig 9: The prices of elementor pro per month and the number of websites it can be used on

Elementor's Free version offers limitless design possibilities. Elementor Pro, however, empowers you with more professional tools that speed up your workflow, and allows you to get more conversions and sales.

How to Build the Homepage of your E-Commerce Site with Elementor

To design the homepage of your e-commerce store using elementor page builder, take the following steps:

-Login to your WordPress admin area

-Open a new tab on in your browser and visit your website

As you open the new tab, just type in your website URL. If am to use the website link of the learning site am using to teach you, I will type www.teachkindle.com in the new tab I opened

Select the "Home" of your e-commerce site

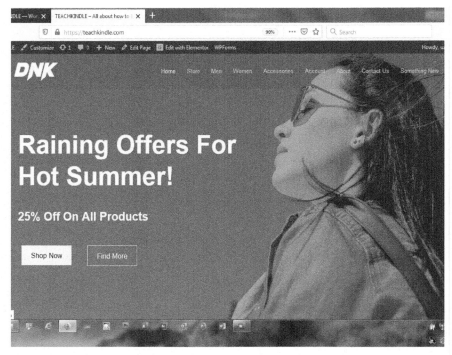

Fig 9.1: Select the "Home" menu item as shown

The Home is the first menu item as shown before "Store" and others. I selected Home first because it is the landing page of the online store. So, I want to design it first with elementor.

-

-Select Edit with Elementor

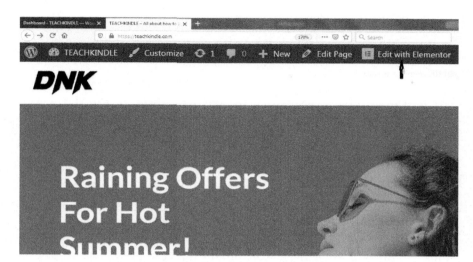

Fig 9.2: Edit with Elementor shown

When you click "Edit with Elementor", it gives you the opportunity to build the homepage with elementor.

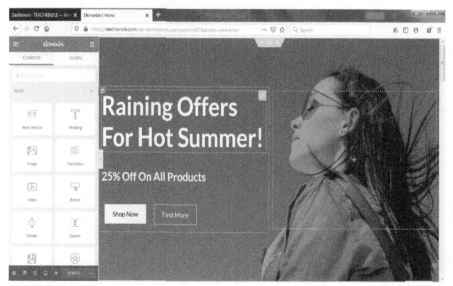

Fig 9.3: Image shows what displayed when I selected Edit with Elementor

-Make changes on the page

Take your cursor to the section you want to make changes, click on that section and elementor editing tools makes it possible for you to make changes. If you want to edit the text on the page, just delete the texts and then type in your own words. As shown in Fig 9.3, I will delete the words that read "Raining Offers For Hot Summer!" and add my own words.

Elementor gives you that opportunity to add any texts you want to use on your website pages. So, do well to type in the texts you want your site visitors and customers to see. You can change texts and images. You can even decide to delete the words and do not have any other words inside. It is your choice to make.

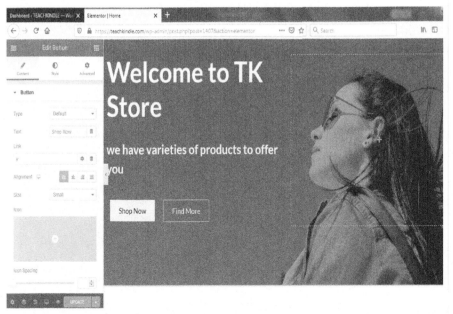

Fig 9.4: The look when I changed the default texts on my "Home"

Using the template am making use of in this teaching, you can make changes on the term "Check Out" and "Shop Now". By default, there is no link added to the buttons. So, if you are using the same Astra Theme, click on the keywords, right click and select Edit. From the elementor tool section, make the changes you want. Add the link you want the customers to be taken to once they click on "Shop Now" or Check Out".

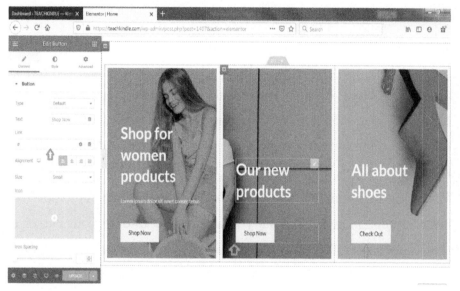

Fig 9.5: Inserting link to direct site visitors to where to buy certain products

You can also change the background picture by taking your cursor to the image and use drag and drop technique if you want to.

-Hit Update button

After you have made the changes to your taste, just hit "Update" button at the bottom part of the elementor editing tools.

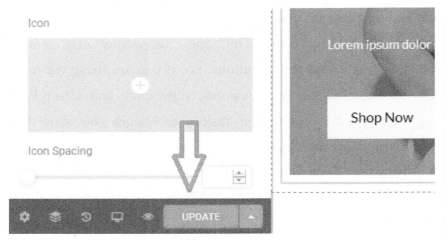

Fig 9.6: The "Update" button shown

Once you click on the Update these changes you made using elementor page builder will be saved. Do not forget to save by clicking on the button otherwise all these designs you made will just be a waste of time and energy.

With this information you can make changes at the footer part of your homepage as well. What you are to do is to drag your cursor to the footer area of your e-commerce site and change the words or images you want to change. At the end of the activity still click on Update to save.

I am thinking of publishing my next book on Elementor and WordPress so you can get it and get deep understanding on the elementor page builder. It is a book you will be proud of getting.

Guide on how to insert or change your E-commerce Site Title, Tagline and Logo

You can decide to make your site title visible or not. But whatever be the case, you can insert title to e-commerce site through WordPress irrespective of the title we inserted when I taught you on how to install WordPress to your domain through control panel.

To insert title to your e-commerce website, do the following:

- Login to your admin dashboard
- Select Appearance
- Select Customize

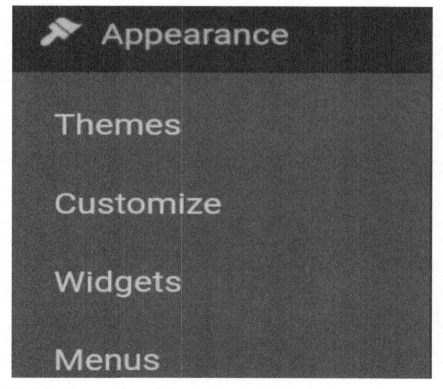

Fig 9.7: The position of Customize as No 2 under Appearance

- Choose "Header"
- Choose Site Identity

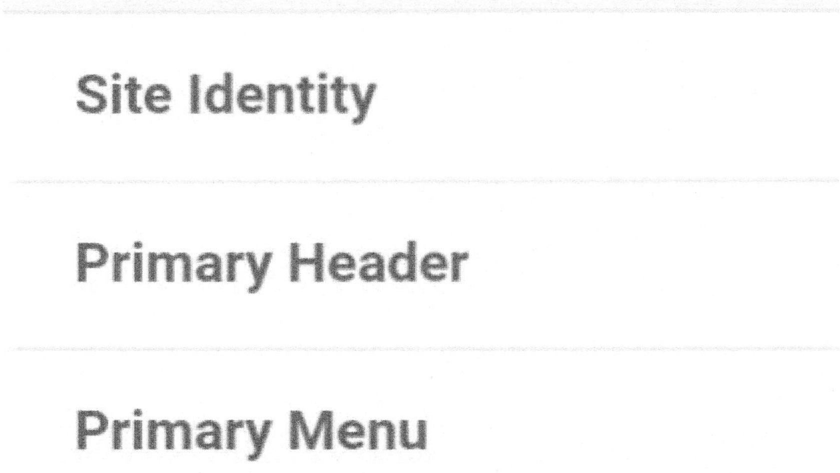

Site Identity

Primary Header

Primary Menu

Fig 9.8: Select the Site Identity option

-Make the changes needed under Site Title and Tagline

SITE TITLE

Site Title

☐ Display Site Title

SITE TAGLINE

Tagline

☐ Display Site Tagline

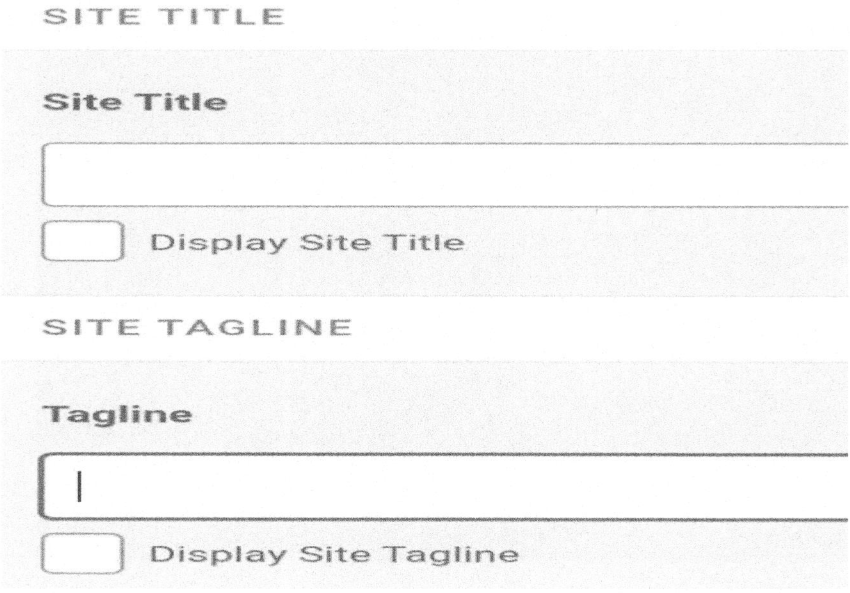

Fig 9.9: The boxes to enter your Site Title and Tagline

Since we want to change the website title and description, just click inside the provided space, erase the words that were there before and type something new which you want as title and site description.

- Check/tick the box "Display Site Title" and "Display Tagline". But when I was handling this section on my e-commerce website, I decided to enter "TK Store" as my Site Title and did not tick the box to "Display Site Title". In the Tagline section, I did not add anything because I included what I supposed to put there on my homepage when I was designing the homepage with elementor.

- Change your Site Logo or Delete it

Drag your cursor up to the site logo section. You are to delete the existing default logo and then upload your own if you wish to use site logo.

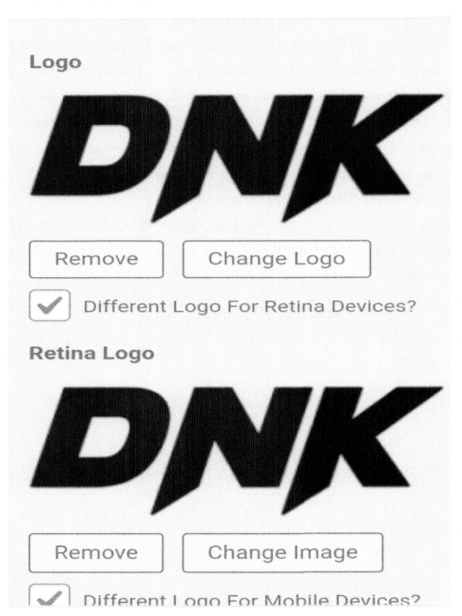

Fig 9.1.1: Default site logo on my e-commerce website

In my own design, I did not use site logo because I did not need it. I am okay with the site tile I chose to use. To remove the default site logo, click on "Remove" and uncheck the box "Different Logo from Mobile Devices" Remove all the logos on the logo section. If you have done this and the logo still shows up on your e-commerce site, then look at the instruction that may show up on top of the logo section and adhere to it.

- Click on Publish on top right corner

When you click on publish, your changes are saved. You can then take a new look at your e-commerce website by visiting the homepage.

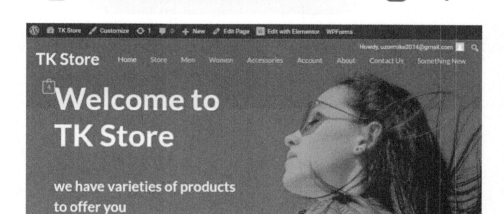

Fig 9.1.2: The new look of my e-commerce website after the changes.

I hope you understand the guide on this section. Do not forget am always available for you to write to.

Chapter 10

How to Market and Promote your E-Commerce Store

One thing is to build an e-commerce website and another thing is to make that website known by people. That is the step that will put money into your bank accounts. When that alert enters your accounts, you smile.

So, in this chapter, I will be teaching you on how to market and promote your created e-commerce site to attract more buyers globally or locally.

Steps to take to Market and Promote your E-Commerce Website

To make your e-commerce website known and selling, I advise you take these steps:

- Register your business
- Have a physical business
- Make your e-commerce site SEO friendly
- Use social media Sites
- Go into paid advertisements
- Start from the people you know

- Advertise on bigger e-commerce websites
- Get people review your products
- Speak about your online store on radio stations and television channels
- Build a team with intelligent entrepreneurs and IT specialists

Register your Business

Avoid any kind of trouble that may come between you and the body in charge of business registration in your country and community. Make sure you register your business with the government approved body in the country where you stay and where you make your sales. This will protect the reputation of your business. It will make people understand that your business is legal and has sound government support.

When you register your business and build it online through e-commerce website, government body will not tag it as illegal. They will confirm it as clearly legal because they already know about its existence due to the registration you have done with them. Do not say you are just starting and therefore there is no need to go and register the business with the government of your country. That is a wrong philosophy.

If you live in United States of America and the business you want to engage in which makes you build an e-commerce website is a small business, you can register that your business name with the state and local government. You can ask of an approved state agent that can help you get the job done in the state you are residing. You can get your trademark name protected through this means.

Creating a Physical Business to gain Online presence

It is not new to hear that many have become victims of online scams in United States and other parts of the world. Sometimes people have doubts of what appears online because of the bad experience their friends had some time ago. So, you need to gain their trust before you see huge sales on your online store.

One of the ways to gain their trust is by having a physical store in that your location. Whenever your physical customers come to buy some products from your physical store, tell them about the online store through which you use in selling the physical products to them. Some of them will be happy to hear that. They will be happy of the drastic step you have taken to get your business online and not just running a brick and mortar kind of business.

Print some fliers and have them inside your brick and mortar business store. When customers come to make purchase physically, give them your fliers which will show what you sell on your online store. Your online store URL (your website link) should be boldly written there.

In the flier, briefly explain how they can place order and then their products get delivered to them in minutes at the comfort of their homes. The guide on how to make the purchase through your e-commerce website can come in this way:

- Visit my e-commerce website at www.shopproducts.com

- Click on "Store" among the menu items

- Select the products you want to buy and add them to cart

- Select "View cart" and then "Proceed to Checkout"

Also ask them for referrals. Believe me, people that love you can sincerely work for you and make sure they give you as many referrals as possible. If they are students, they will take it upon themselves to start preaching the good news to their fellow students. They can start like this "hello my fellow students, please I want to tell you guys about my friend that owns an e-commerce website in this same city.

She can deliver your ordered products within minutes because she lives close to us. Her products are of good quality because I have been buying from her. Please visit her website at www.shopproducts.com."

With this kind of mouth to masses advertisement by your already existing customers, it will not take much time for your e-commerce website to start growing in that city. With time, it expands to other parts of the country where your shop is located. Many e-commerce websites have grown through this kind of marketing.

Build SEO friendly E-commerce Site to gain Online presence

Nobody feels happy browsing through a sluggish website not even an e-commerce website. In fact, it will be more annoying to browse through a sluggish e-commerce site. Do not make that mistake because you are the one that needs the customers. Customers can leave your e-commerce website out of annoyance because of the sluggishness in loading the pages of the website.

Have you felt headache because you were browsing through a sluggish website? If you have not, it has happened to me. At a point I got tired because I was running out of time to do what I wanted to do. At the end I closed the page and sourced for the information I needed through another website.

Having a website that is not SEO friendly can make your website to rank low among others. It will make search engines to see your website as a substandard one. And when this happen, people will regard your website as a weak one. When people search for products using search engine like Google, even though you have such product on your e-commerce store, it will not display on the first pages of Google search results because your e-commerce site is not SEO friendly. Before going further in this section, let me enlighten you on what SEO implies.

SEO stands for Search engine optimization. It is the process of growing the quality and quantity of website traffic by increasing the visibility of a website or a web page to users of a web search engine. SEO refers to the improvement of unpaid results (known as "natural" or "organic" results) and excludes direct traffic and the purchase of paid placement. If you do not have deep idea on how to make your e-commerce website to have good SEO, you can hire SEO experts in your location to help you achieve a good one.

Sometimes the hosting company you used in building your website can be a contributor to how your website behaves in terms of SEO. I will recommend you host with Go Daddy or Ipage when building a practical e-commerce website for your online business. The speed of their page loading is okay. As you host your e-commerce website, pay for dedicated server and not shared one.

Also, avoid installing and activating some unnecessarily plugins in your site while building. If you know that having large number of sliders on your e-commerce site is not that important, just avoid having them in large number on your webpages. Sliders can slow loading of many website pages.

Promoting a site to increase the number of backlinks, or inbound links, is another SEO tactic. By May 2015, mobile search had surpassed desktop search. So, make your site to be mobile friend. People visit Websites on the go these days. They do not need to go home and use their desktops before they can visit websites any longer. In your website settings, make it to be mobile friendly so that people can browse through it easily using their mobile phones.

The impact of Social Media Sites on Promotion of Online Stores

Social media has good impact in the promotion of e-commerce websites. If you are the owner of a particular online store, you can use social media sites to tell the masses what your e-commerce website is all about. You can also broadcast messages to your friends and followers telling them to buy from your site and encourage their friends to buy from your online store.

Example of social media sites that have helped promote some online stores are Facebook, Twitter, Instagram, and LinkedIn. You can have message like "Hi friends, I newly launch an e-commerce website. Please buy from my online store with the link "www.myonlinestore.com" and tell your friends". When you have this kind of message on your wall and also broadcast it as a message to your contacts, some contacts can call you to confirm the information and at the end buy from your online store. Do not underestimate the power of social media sites in marketing and promotion of e-commerce stores.

When you create a page, you can invite all your friends to like your page on social media. Also solicit for referrals from them to like your page. Do not forget to update information on your social media page and sample any new products you have on your store for interested persons to go and buy.

Whatsapp Mobile application is another important tool to use. Your contacts that know you well can see the products you sell on your online store directly when you upload them on your status.

If you have any celebrity in your list of friends or those you are following on any social media platform, they can be a source of boost to you. You can communicate with them and plead that they help you broadcast your online store through their pages.

If any of them agrees and decide to do it for you in as much that the person in question is a "big celebrity" with many followers, forget it your life has changed in a positive sense. They do have rich people as followers. Those followers can buy good number of products from you. And when they get use to your store, you can start selling thousands of products every day. I know of someone who sold many of her products in a day because a celebrity decided to sample her products on his Instagram page, and he pleaded to the followers to buy from her.

Marketing your E-commerce Site by paid Advertisements

This method has proven worth the invested money for the past years. Paid advertising is an advertising method whereby a person (in this teaching an e-commerce website owner) pays an online advertising company to show their commodities, companies or services to internet users with the targeting aim of creating awareness or making sells. Targeted online adverts have made some entrepreneurs and companies have good online popularity among internet users.

A form of paid advertising is the one called Pay-Per-Click (PPC). Pay-per-click (PPC) is an internet advertising model used to drive traffic to websites, in which an advertiser pays a publisher (typically a search engine, website owner, or a network of websites) when the ad is clicked.

Pay-per-click is commonly associated with first-tier search engines (such as Google Ads, Amazon Advertising, and Microsoft Advertising formerly Bing Ads, Facebook, Twitter, LinkedIn and Instagram). With search engines, advertisers typically bid on keyword phrases relevant to their target market and pay when ads (text-based search ads or shopping ads that are a combination of images and text) are clicked.

The good thing about paid advertising is that you choose any amount to pay per click on any image or text that you use to advertise your e-commerce website. When internet users click on any of your ads, they are directed to your e-commerce website. There can be few words on the image that will get their attention to click on the ads that will end up taking them to your website. Example can be "Get this quality shoes from ShopSound". In the example, I assumed "ShopSound" as the name of the e-commerce website.

Visit BlogsBunny.com

We showcase only the best news and media content from across the world

Fig 10: Advert placed on webpage by Google which encourages readers to visit a particular site.

Paid online advertising is not much money demanding if you want to cover a particular location. You can pay as low as $0.05 per click on the advert you place on any website.

If you signed up for paid advertising with Google for example, they show internet users adverts that mainly relate to what they search for on the internet. Their machine of the advert company is power in detecting that which internet users browse about on the internet. Take for example that an internet user usually browses online about latest shoes in United States, when you sign up with Google for them to show people ads on what you sell on your e-commerce site, the moment the user searches about the latest shoes in United States and you sell shoes on your e-commerce website, it is possible that Google will display ads that will direct the user to your website when he clicks on it. The reason is because you sell shoes on your site and the person searched on the product.

How to Advertise your E-Commerce Site with Google (Google Ads)

It was called Google AdWords before now, but it was changed to Google Ads in July 24, 2018. It is an online advertising platform developed by Google, where advertisers pay to display brief advertisements, service offerings, product listings, video content, and generate mobile application installs within the Google ad network to web users.

To register your e-commerce website on Google Ads, follow these steps:

- Signup on Google Ads through the link "https://ads.google.com"

- Establish your account goals

- Determine your audience

- Conduct keyword research

- Set budgets and bids

- Build your optimal account structure

- Write high-performing ads

- Create effective landing pages

- Implement conversion tracking

- Grow your remarketing lists

- Make optimization a habit

How to Advertise your E-commerce site on Facebook

As at the first quarter of the year 2020, Facebook has over 2.6 billion monthly active users. With this statistic, you can target active users in your location that you want to sell your products to through your e-commerce website.

To signup for Facebook Ads as an advertiser, take the following steps:

- Step 1. Choose your objective

Log into Facebook Ads Manager and select the Campaigns tab, then click Create to get started with a new Facebook ad campaign.

- Step 2. Name your campaign

- Step 3. Set up your ad account

- Step 4. Target your audience

- Step 5. Choose your Facebook ad placements

- Step 6. Set your budget and schedule

- Step 7. Create your ad

Promoting your E-commerce Site from known to unknown people

When a young person is given the job of a marketer in bank or insurance company, one of the instructions he is given to win businesses is to start from the people he knows to the ones he does not know. In the other words, he should start from the known to the unknown. Are you familiar with that statement when you were taught algebra in your secondary school? It still applies when you want to promote your e-commerce website.

Who are your family members? Where are your cousins, uncles and aunts? I believe they know you and want you to grow even as you want to make impact in life.

Since they are all part of you and will feel happy to see you succeed, then talk to them. Tell them about your e-commerce website. Tell them what you sell on that your online store and how to place order. It is easier to convince people who are close to you than those that are far from you. Because of this, start with them first.

When I got a job of marketing some time ago in an insurance company, I began with the people I know. I started with my elder sister from her to known friends. Those known friends and my relations later connected me to their other relations and friends. From there I began to meet the unknown. That helped my growth in the insurance company then. Start from those people you know and tell them about that your e-commerce site that you established to do business.

Advertising on bigger E-commerce Websites

Sometimes it is good to stand on the shoulders of giants to see far. Even before you established your e-commerce site, there were bigger e-commerce sites that has been in existence. Those sites can be referred to as giants because they have been existing. People have known them for some time and because of that are popular.

But you can't say that because there are big e-commerce sites in your country, you do not need to build your own. You cannot say that because life is filled with competition. You enter the market no matter what and compete with others. You can build your own brand as time progresses.

Even as big as amazon.com e-commerce website is, there are still some other e-commerce sites in the same country which are doing well in their own capacity. You can think of state location of your own site to take advantage of the shipping fee. If Amazon ships from Washington for example, you can decide to have your store in California and target buyers around there.

Advertising on big e-commerce sites can make people know about the existence of your online store. When people buy from those sites, they can see your advert that may read "You can still buy from TK Store". When they click on the advert link, they are directed to your site. Who knows if they will see other nice products on your platform and buy them? It is a way you can use to market your store to online shoppers. You pay per click on those your ads.

Getting People review your Products

Review has been one of the actions that attract buyers or discourage them from buying products from e-commerce sites. When products receive positive reviews, it motivates others to buy more of such products. But when products receive negative reviews from buyers, it scares other prospective buyers away from purchasing them.

Positive reviews have proven to be helpful in making products sell more. In Amazon for instance, books with many negative reviews hardly sell further. In fact, it is a way of sending such books to their early graves. It is better the books did not receive any review at all than to get many negative ones.

Most buyers are always in a haste to buy from online stores and walk away. They are not that patient to come back after buying to leave positive reviews under the products they purchased. Even if the products are very sound, they see going back to the store to write review under the purchased product as a waste of time.

Because some customers are not interested in living any review on some products they will buy from your online store, it is now your responsibility to do the job. Contact customers that you have good relationship with, and you know bought some products from your online store. Plead to them to go back to the store, login to their accounts through the store and write good review under the product they bought from your shop.

That is a good promotional technique. When people view that same product and begin to contemplate on whether that product will be good when delivered to them, the positive reviews under that product will motivate them to buy the product.

Advertising your Store through Radio and Television Channels

Imagine that feeling when people are seated in their homes watching a particular television channel and you appear to speak on the television channel. You introduce yourself as the Chief Executive Officer of "tkproducts.com" and they are like "wow". "So, this the CEO of the newly launched e-commerce website?", some will say. "He is handsome and looks cool, I will make my first purchase from his site tomorrow". "He must be tech savvy to be able to create such beautiful platform". All will be similar sentences coming from the television viewers.

With such kind of statements and exposure, you start getting people's attention. You are getting their attention because you have had some exposure to large numbers of people. People may like you for the fact that they have seen your picture appear on the screen of their televisions. That builds their trust and make them believe that your store is real.

In speaking to the masses through television channels, with screen narration, guide them step by step on how to buy from the site. Also assure them on security. Let them know that their details including their card details is safe and secure. With this assurance, they will make bold step and start buying and you grow your earnings as well.

Another approach to promote your store is speaking to people through radio stations. You can just buy 15 minutes from the station just to talk on your e-commerce website and the products you offer. Do not forget to tell them about the benefit they will gain from buying from you. The reduced cost of shipping and shipping within 48 hours of order is a good selling technique. So put that into consideration as you speak to the masses. Television and radio advertising have really impacted on e-commerce stores positively.

Building a Team with Intelligent Entrepreneurs and IT Specialists

I believe you have not forgotten that saying that "two good heads are better than one"? You may have a good idea but if you build a team, your ideas added to their own ideas can make it sound and solid. When people with like minds agree to do something and they execute it, they are likely to succeed more. So, building a team with other entrepreneurs will help you promote your e-commerce website. You can take your plan to entrepreneurs in your location who do not have their own e-commerce sites. Tell them about how you people can make more money when you work together. Also, let them see the benefit in it. In fact, building a team with them can expand the quantity and quality of products you have in your store.

And another benefit is that as you talk to people about your online store, they also help in the growth of the store as they themselves talk to people they know to buy from your store. After sales in every week, you people will share profit and continue with the site promotion. If your e-commerce website is targeting a particular country or location, because of your team, you people may start shipping internationally with time. The reason is because you people will have joint capital to do that.

You can meet few people who are good in Information Technology (IT) to help maintain your online store. These persons must be people you can trust so that they do not compromise anything on your store. In case you site is down and your store not loading well, the IT specialists search for the solution and get that fixed. You can hire young graduates from IT related department to work with the few specialists and help reinforce the team.

Young graduates from IT departments can easily get update on what is new in online store performance. With this kind of information, they can use them in helping your e-commerce website grow. As this happen, your store will be more discoverable and hence rank high in search results through search engine.

Promoting your e-commerce sites involves some tasks. These are all practical tasks that those who are doing well in e-commerce business are using to break grounds. Take my advice in prompting your e-commerce business as explained in this chapter. It will help you grow your e-commerce business.